# GETTING ALONG WITH EACH OTHER

## RICHARD L. STRAUSS

ECS
MINISTRIES
*The Word to the World*

*Getting Along with Each Other*

Richard L. Strauss

Published by:
ECS Ministries
PO Box 1028
Dubuque, IA 52004-1028
phone: (563) 585-2070
email: ecsorders@ecsministries.org
website: www.ecsministries.org

First Printed 2010

ISBN 978-1-59387-123-9

Code: B-GAEO

Copyright © 2010 ECS Ministries

Cover and text design by LambCreek, www.lambcreek.com

This book was originally published by Here's Life Publishers, Inc., PO Box 1576, San Bernardino, CA, 92402. Copyright © 1985 by Here's Life Publishers, Inc.

*Printed in the United States of America*

# TABLE OF
# CONTENTS

# 1

# BROKEN
# FRIENDSHIPS

WOULDN'T IT BE GREAT if we Christians could always get along with each other? We have so much in common—one Lord, the Lord Jesus Christ; one revealed Word from Him; one body of which we are all members; one common desire to glorify Christ; one common goal to share Him with others. And yet we seem to have a reputation for misunderstandings, disagreements, dissension, and division.

We've all witnessed little cliques, gossip, and hard feelings between Christians. We're all aware of church splits, the formation of new denominations, and the proliferation of para-church organizations that often overlap in their aims and purposes. We've all observed crumbling marriages among professing Christians. We must admit that Christians do not always get along very well with one another. How can it be?

I would like to explore that question by examining an intense disagreement between two great and godly men in Scripture. These men were close friends and fellow workers. It was a disagreement that resulted in the parting of their paths and the fracturing of their friendship. It is not a pretty story. In fact, it is rather sad. It never should have happened.

**God uses us despite our weaknesses.**

But I, for one, am glad it did, and I am pleased that God saw fit to include the account of it in His Word. It helps us to know that the great heroes of the faith were human, just like us. When we see what God did through them *despite* their weaknesses, we know there is hope for us. And by examining their mistakes, we will also see how to maintain harmonious relations with our own fellow workers.

## A Genuine Friendship

Their relationship began in earnest when a great number of Gentiles in Syrian Antioch came to know Christ through the preaching of refugees from Jerusalem (Acts 11:19–21). This turn of events disturbed some of the leaders of the church in Jerusalem. They were not ready to accept Gentiles into the fellowship of the church, and they wanted to send someone to Antioch to investigate the situation. Barnabas was their obvious choice. He was a Jew (of the tribe of Levi), so he knew the law and understood the Hebrew mind. He was raised on the island of Cyprus, so he spoke Greek, understood the Gentile mind, and would not inadvertently offend them. He was highly regarded as a good man, generous, gracious, and godly (Acts 4:36–37).

It proved to be the right choice. Barnabas remained there, and the work in Antioch prospered. "Then when he arrived and witnessed the grace of God, he rejoiced and began to encourage them all with resolute heart to remain true to the Lord; for he was a good man, and full of the Holy Spirit and of faith. And considerable numbers were brought to the Lord" (Acts 11:23–24). The work prospered to such a degree that Barnabas could not handle it by himself any longer. The believers in that local church were too young in the Lord to be elevated to positions of leadership, so his only recourse was to reach outside for help.

He knew just the man. As far as we know, he had first met Saul of Tarsus in Jerusalem three years after Saul's supernatural conversion on the Damascus road. Everybody else in Jerusalem was afraid that Saul had come to spy on them and lay plans for his next attack against them. But Barnabas believed in him. He reached out to him, encouraged other leaders in Jerusalem to accept him (Acts 9:26–29), and a genuine friendship was born. After those days in Jerusalem, Saul returned to his home town of Tarsus, from which he penetrated all the surrounding Gentile areas with the gospel. Word kept filtering back of his powerful ministry (Gal. 1:23). Saul of Tarsus was the man Barnabas needed in Antioch. "And he left for Tarsus to look for Saul; and when he had found him, he brought him to Antioch. And for an entire year they met with the church and taught considerable numbers; and the disciples were first called Christians in Antioch" (Acts 11:25–26). A great team ministry was born.

Together they served the Lord with great blessing. They seemed to fit together and complement each other well. When the church in Antioch decided to send relief money to the famine-stricken Christians in Jerusalem, Barnabas and Saul delivered it together (Acts 11:30). Together they returned to Antioch (12:25), where three others had been added to the staff (13:1). But Barnabas and Saul continued to serve the Lord there, together.

When the Holy Spirit gave directions for the first organized foreign missionary thrust, we're not surprised to hear Him say, "Set apart for Me Barnabas and Saul for the work to which I have called them" (13:2). Thus they entered a new venture together. It was a fruitful ministry of evangelism and church planting— a magnificent spiritual success. What a team! They returned to Antioch to report what God had done and then continued to minister there, together (Acts 14:26–28).

When the false doctrine of salvation by works began to infiltrate the church, these two men stood against it, together (Acts 15:2a). When it was decided to send representatives to Jerusalem to confer with the apostles and elders about the problem, these two men were asked to go, together (Acts 15:2b). Together, they declared what wonders God had done among the Gentiles (15:12). And when a decision was reached and a letter was sent from the apostles and elders to the churches, it said, "It seemed good to us, having become of one mind, to select men to send to you with our beloved Barnabas and Paul, men who have risked their lives for the name of our Lord Jesus Christ" (Acts 15:25–26). "Our beloved Barnabas and Paul!" That about says it all. They were genuine friends whose team ministry had brought great blessing to the church and inspired great admiration and affection. When they finished their assignment, they returned to Antioch and continued teaching and preaching the Word of God, together (Acts 15:35).

> **Many things can strain our relationships— things we may easily overlook.**

## A Growing Tension

Two things happened during those years of team ministry which may have put a strain on their relationship—things we may easily overlook. First, the leadership of the team changed hands. There is no question that Barnabas was the original leader. He was the first shepherding leader of the church of Antioch. He held the respect of the people there. He personally brought Paul in to help with the ministry. His name consistently appears first in those early years for a reason. When the five members of the group of workers are listed in Acts 13:1, his name is first, Saul's last. The Holy Spirit put him first in the call to missionary service (Acts 13:2), and he is still listed first as the journey progressed (Acts 13:7). He was the recognized leader.

But something happened on that journey. Away from the environment of Antioch where Barnabas was the recognized leader, Saul (now called Paul) began to assume the lead. His stronger personality and more prominent gifts seemed to make it a natural thing. He was the one who confronted a sorcerer named Elymas and kept him from further hindering the gospel (Acts 13:9–12). By the time they finished their ministry on Cyprus, Luke called the team "Paul and his companions" (13:13). It was now "The Apostle Paul Evangelistic Association." That was quite a change, and rather sudden.

Paul's leadership was even more evident in the synagogue at Pisidia (13:15–16). We hear no protests from Barnabas, nor do we see any outward indication of bitterness, resentment, or hard feeling. But we must wonder if deep in his soul Barnabas did not feel a little hurt about it. Did he think Paul came on a little too strong, that he insisted on having things his way, that he failed to consider the feelings of others? If so, did he ever mention it to Paul?

The second incident that put a strain on their relationship was an isolated occurrence at Antioch shortly after the council at Jerusalem. We learn nothing about it in Acts, but Paul tells us about it years later in his epistle to the Galatians. Peter was visiting the church at Antioch and had conducted himself just as Paul and Barnabas did, without prejudice against the Gentile Christians. He entered freely into social contacts with them, ate with them, and fellowshipped with them without restraint.

But when a group of Jewish Christians arrived from Jerusalem and expressed alarm over Peter's behavior, he backed away and stopped eating with the Gentiles. While social equality was taken for granted in Antioch, it was still not accepted by these Judaizers, and Peter was afraid of the trouble they might cause him back home in Jerusalem. Paul called it hypocrisy. And he was right. That is exactly what it was.

But the thing that hurt Paul most was that his dear friend Barnabas allowed himself to be affected by Peter's hypocrisy.

Paul later wrote, "The rest of the Jews joined him in hypocrisy, with the result that even Barnabas was carried away by their hypocrisy" (Gal. 2:13).

Can you feel the emotion in those words, "even Barnabas"? Paul could not believe it. How could Barnabas do that? He knew better. He understood the doctrines of grace, Christian liberty, and the oneness of all true believers in Christ. He had been treating the Gentile believers in Antioch as equals for years. Now, for fear of what a few Judaizers might say about him in Jerusalem, he turned coward and left Paul standing alone. Could it have been Barnabas's hurt over the change in leadership that made him turn his back on Paul so easily?

Barnabas surely recognized his mistake and repented.

The wound would heal, but the scar would remain, leaving a strain on their friendship. I wonder if deep in his soul Paul did not harbor a bit of mistrust for Barnabas. Maybe he thought he was a bit wishy-washy, a compromiser. His mention of it in his letter to the Galatians reveals that he never really forgot it. Did they ever talk it out, or did they just ignore it and hope everything would be okay (as we so often do).

## A Great Disagreement

If the feelings were there, and Paul and Barnabas never owned up to them, honestly admitted them, or openly discussed them, surely the stage was set for a violent disagreement. And that is exactly what happened a very short time later. Chronologically, the next turn of events in their relationship occurred immediately after Barnabas's hypocritical actions at Antioch.

"After some days Paul said to Barnabas, 'Let us return and visit the brethren in every city in which we proclaimed the word of the Lord, and see how they are.' Barnabas wanted to take John, called Mark, along with them also. But Paul kept insisting that they should not take him along who had deserted them in Pamphylia and had not gone with them to the work" (Acts 15:36–38).

It was a simple procedural matter. It seems so inconsequential; we would think that they could have sat down together, discussed the pros and cons, and come to a mutually agreeable decision. For example, "Let's not take him on this trip, but maybe on the next one." Or, "Maybe we can take him, but we should lay down certain prerequisites ahead of time." Or, "Let's talk to him about his previous defection and the seriousness of it, find out what was behind it and how we can avoid it next time." Certainly, some mutually agreeable solution could have been found.

But agreeable solutions are not usually found when unresolved feelings are already running deep. We have been hurt, and our hurt may have settled into a lingering, low-grade anger that we are probably not even willing to admit to ourselves. And now, even a minor disagreement becomes a major issue to us. We say to ourselves, "I'm not going to let him do that to me again. I'm going to take my stand right here, and I'm not backing down. If I let him take advantage of me this time, there's no telling what he'll try to do next."

The Scripture says, "And there occurred such a sharp disagreement that they separated from one another, and Barnabas took Mark with him and sailed away to Cyprus. But Paul chose Silas and left, being committed by the brethren to the grace of the Lord" (Acts 15:39–40). The Greek word for "sharp disagreement" is the basis for the English word *paroxysm,* which means "a sudden violent emotion or action." There is no way to whitewash this dispute. It was not just a mild difference of opinion. This was a serious argument. Emotions erupted. Sharp words were exchanged. Maybe unkind accusations were hurled. The word involves irritation and anger.

> **Solutions are not usually found when unresolved feelings are already running deep.**

## Three Reasons

This kind of contention occurs regularly among Christians—husbands and wives, parents and children, members of church congregations. Friendships have been broken, families torn apart, churches split. What are the reasons? One is *pride.* We may be sure that our opinions are right and others' opinions are wrong. If our opinions are rejected, we may think that somehow reflects on our worth as persons. So we fight with every weapon at our disposal to win the argument and protect our standing.

Another reason is *inadequate information.* We may be too quick to judge others. We form opinions on the basis of a few isolated experiences, or we believe somebody else's assessment of them and then jump to conclusions about them and their motives. Once our judgment is formed, we tend to view almost everything else they say or do in that light and use it to confirm our preconceived and prejudicial opinions. That can lead to repeated misunderstandings. We assume that because someone's motives were wrong in the past, they must be wrong now. We refuse to believe that people can grow and change.

But one of the most common reasons for contention among believers is our notorious *lack of communication,* especially failure to share our feelings. We find that it is easier to accuse, reprimand, or condemn others for what they have done, to argue over trivialities, or insist on our own way, than it is to admit honestly our feelings of hurt, insecurity, inferiority, anxiety, fear, selfishness, or jealousy. We do not want to look bad, so we cover up those feelings.

**We need to admit to our feelings and talk about them.**

If we want to avoid angry arguments like this, there are some things we will need to do. The first is to learn to admit to our feelings and to talk about them. "I felt hurt when you did that. But I want things to be right between us. Can we talk about it?" "I felt put down when you said that. Would you explain to me what you meant?" When we refuse to talk, and instead let the hard feelings seethe, the explosions are sure to come. Don't put it off. Talk! Openly and honestly! Not about what the other person has done wrong, but about what you are feeling. There is no evidence that Paul and Barnabas did that.

Another thing we need to do is to allow for differences of opinion. God did not make us all from the same mold. We have different backgrounds and we think differently about things. If God can accept all of us with our differences, certainly we can learn to accept each other. On clear biblical issues, we cannot compromise. But most issues are not matters of right or wrong. We cannot say dogmatically that either Paul or Barnabas was right or wrong. The church seems to have put its official sanction on Paul (Acts 15:40), but that does not mean the church refused to approve Barnabas. It simply means that Paul was recognized as the leader now, even at Antioch. The rest of the story in Acts is about Paul, but that was only proper since he was the leading figure in the church. The Spirit of God does not tell us who was right or wrong.

> None of us is perfect. We need to be willing to forgive.

Paul had a point. It is disheartening when someone on whom you are depending lets you down as Mark did. But Barnabas had a good point also. None of us is perfect; not Paul, not Peter, not Barnabas, not Mark, nor anybody else. Everybody deserves an opportunity to prove himself. The question is not, "Who is right or who is wrong?" But rather, "How can we work together in Christian love to do the job God has committed to us?" God wants us to learn the grace of forbearance for one another. Paul and Barnabas seem to have lost it.

One more thing—be quick to forgive. We are all human. We are going to let our old sin natures and psychological hang-ups get the best of us at times, and we are going to say the wrong things in the wrong way. We need to be patient and understanding with each other and willing to forgive. We all do foolish things once in awhile. We want people to forgive us when we do, so we will need to extend the same courtesy to them. Paul and Barnabas failed on all of these counts.

## A Good End

The most encouraging part of this story is the assurance that our sovereign God is in control of the whole situation.

Satan was at work, sin natures were flaring, but God is omnipotent. He could have changed the circumstances somehow to circumvent the conflict, but He permitted it, and He did what He always does for those who love Him: He worked it together to achieve good.

For one thing, it became a growing experience for the people involved, particularly for Paul. He was given to strong reactions (see Acts 23:3; also 17:16 where the verb form of the same word, "sharp disagreement," is used). But God was working on this weakness in him. Some time later he wrote that love "is not easily provoked" (1 Corinthians 13:5, KJV, and again, he used the verb form of the same word). Maybe, when he wrote those words, he was reflecting back to this unhappy occasion. The argument helped him see his weakness and to claim God's power to love.

> **God can find a way to use even our stupid and selfish blunders to glorify Himself.**

Another beneficial thing God did through the conflict was to send out two missionary teams instead of one. While this was not the best way to accomplish that goal, maybe it would not have been achieved any other way. So while the argument itself did not glorify God, the ultimate result did. God can do that for us, too. He can find a way to use even our stupid and selfish blunders to glorify Himself. That is no excuse for sinning, but it certainly encourages us as we remember the blunders we have made.

One of the most obvious and important results of the disagreement was that a life was salvaged for God's usefulness. Only God knows what would have happened to Mark if Barnabas had not taken him under his spiritual supervision and nurtured him in his faith. Even Paul later admitted that Mark was profitable to him for ministry (2 Tim. 4:11). It is encouraging to know that God can use *our* mistakes, as well, to accomplish something beneficial in our lives or in the lives of others.

While there is no evidence that Paul and Barnabas ever resumed the kind of close relationship they once had, the bitterness was washed away and they came to respect one another deeply again. Paul later spoke kindly and admiringly of Barnabas (1 Cor. 9:6). I am confident that there has been a grand reunion in heaven.

But for ourselves, let's not wait until then. Let's learn to be open and honest with each other about our feelings right now, to talk more freely about them, to accept and love one another even when we differ, to avoid judging other people's motives, to tolerate one another's differing opinions, and to forgive one another quickly when old sin natures do hurtful things. Then marriages will be healed, friendships restored, feuding Christians reconciled, churches strengthened, and God glorified.

# 2

# BITS AND
# BEAMS

CRITICISM IS ALMOST A WAY OF LIFE in today's society. We have music critics, art critics, and drama critics. We have critics of government, critics of business, and critics of labor. When a new United States president takes office, it is usually understood that he gets a short honeymoon and then the critics begin to unleash their barrage again, and the normal pattern resumes. We seem to be obsessed with the weaknesses and mistakes of others. We believe our criticism will encourage others to strive for excellence.

Unfortunately, we bring that same mentality into the family. We try to remake our mates and shape up our children by criticism. We Christians may carry that same way of life into the church as well. We pick at other Christians who do not measure up to our expectations, and we find fault with our leaders for not doing things the way we want them done. And we keep telling ourselves that it is the right thing to do. It will make them strive for excellence.

But at some point in our Christian experience we confront the words of our Lord Jesus Christ in the Sermon on the Mount about criticism (Matt. 7:1–5), and we are faced with a decision. Shall we go on as we always have, or shall we change our way of living in this matter to conform to His will? Let's look at the command itself, the caution He added, and the contradiction we face if we disobey.

## The Command

The command is short and simple, just three words—"Do not judge." What does it mean? The word *judge* has the idea of distinguishing or choosing. A judge observes the evidence, evaluates it, and then comes to a certain conclusion. That can be quite positive. It might mean commendation, approval, or exoneration. And even negative judgment is necessary at times. In this very passage, Jesus indicates that the person whose life is pure can help take the speck out of his brother's eye (v. 5). That is a form of judgment with which we will deal in the next chapter on "mending nets" (helping a fellow believer overcome his faults).

In the next verse (v. 6) Jesus says, "Do not give what is holy to dogs, and do not throw your pearls before swine, or they will trample them under their feet, and turn and tear you to pieces." Christ is using dogs and swine to describe profane people who treat spiritual matters with contempt. In order to obey that verse, we obviously have to make a judgment. We must decide who the dogs and swine are. On another occasion Jesus said, "Do not judge according to appearance, but judge with righteous judgment" (John 7:24). This was a command to judge fairly and on the basis of truth and fact rather than by outward appearances, but nevertheless to judge. Is Jesus contradicting Himself? Obviously not; what, then, did He mean?

Most Bible commentators are agreed that in the Matthew passage, Jesus is warning us about a fault-finding spirit, a negative attitude that causes us to pick at others for the things we do not like in them, to accuse them, blame them, and complain to them because they do not live up to our expectations. This preoccupation with faults expresses itself in a twofold way: First, we are inclined to emphasize the *faults* of others rather than their strengths. Second, we are inclined to emphasize the faults of *others* rather than our own. The one word that sums it up is *criticism*. Why did Jesus tell us not to emphasize the faults of others? Was He assuming that most of us have a tendency to do it?

As omniscient God as well as fully man, the Lord Jesus Christ knew the hearts of His audience, and those people represented His wider audience—us. He knows that we all need this reminder to some degree. It is one of the most common sins among Christians, our favorite indoor (and maybe outdoor) sport. I remember reading a story about an Ozark hound sitting in a country store howling, as hounds often do.

> **Jesus is warning us about a fault-finding spirit.**

A stranger walked in and said to the storekeeper, "What's the matter with the dog?"

"He's sitting on a cocklebur," came the reply.

"Why doesn't he get off?"

"Because he'd rather holler."

I am afraid there are Christians like that. They find great satisfaction in hollering at others about the things they do not like. Why do we do that?

The most common reason is probably selfishness. What other people do sometimes inconveniences us, costs us time and money, runs counter to our preferences, or disagrees with our time-honored way of doing things. We want things to be smooth, pleasant, and agreeable for *us,* so we find fault with people who make them otherwise. For example, I may have plans for the evening, but when I get home from work my wife does not have dinner ready. I criticize her for poorly organizing her time because that late dinner takes time away from what I want to do. We may criticize a roommate for leaving the bathroom a mess, because we think we have to clean it up. We may criticize a preacher because he does not organize his sermons as we would like, causing us to work harder to follow his train of thought.

Another reason for criticism could be our own inferiority, which surfaces in the form of pride. Attacking someone else is flattering to ourselves; it gives us a feeling of superiority. If we can show others where they fail to measure up, it makes us feel as if we are a little smarter or better than they are in that area. When we criticize our spouses, we are saying basically, "I'm not as bad as you seem to think. In fact, I may be better than you." In an excellent study on the meaning of love, Dr. Ed Wheat wrote, "Remember, you can never enhance or rekindle the emotions of love by heaping a sense of failure on your partner. I cannot overemphasize this. Never in the slightest way put a feeling of guilt upon your mate."[1] And again, ". . . overlook mistakes and never criticize."[2] That's good advice. It is exactly what Jesus said: "Don't judge."

**When we criticize, we play God.**

## Three Reasons Criticism Is Foolish

Have you ever wondered why criticism is such a foolish habit? For one thing, *our knowledge of others is only partial.* We do not know all the facts. We may not know why they said or did what we are criticizing. We do not know the kind of pressures they are facing, the influences that molded them into the people they are, the force of the temptation that was placed in their path, the motives that prompted their actions. Only God knows all the facts and can come to an accurate evaluation, so He is the only one who has the right to criticize. When we do it, we play God.

For another thing, *our judgment is fallible.* Even if we knew all the facts, we might not interpret them correctly. We are human beings who carry around our own peculiar bundle of biases through which we view the facts. Members of the same jury, for instance, can hear the same facts in a court of law yet they may come to totally opposite conclusions. Only God can interpret all facts accurately. So He is the only one who has the right to criticize. When we do it, we play God.

A third reason criticism is foolish is that *we are not responsible for the actions of other people.* We are not their masters. Paul wrote, "Who are you to judge the servant of another? To his own master he stands or falls" (Rom. 14:4).

> **We seldom grow while we are sulking.**

We are only responsible for our own actions. "So then each one of us will give account of himself to God. Therefore let us not judge one another anymore . . ." (Rom. 14:12–13). When we do it, we play God.

A fourth reason criticism is so foolish is that *it tears down rather than builds up.* When aimed at us, it seldom makes us want to change for the better; it has, instead, the opposite effect. It causes us to defend ourselves, to justify our actions, to try to prove that we are not as bad as we are accused of being. That sabotages our spiritual growth. Criticism also leads to discouragement and self-pity. We feel sorry for ourselves because we think we will never be able to please our critic and because we have to suffer this unjust accusation from him. We seldom grow while we are sulking.

*Criticism also tears down relationships.* It alienates people and builds walls between them. I find criticism unpleasant, so my tendency is to avoid the people who level it. Some husbands and wives avoid each other for that very reason and their marriages are disintegrating as a result. They have developed the habit of criticizing the way each other looks or talks, and the things each other does or does not do. As a result, the husband may stay late at work, then flee to the yard or workshop for refuge when he returns home. The wife spends more and more time with friends and neighbors or finds other outside interests to occupy her attention. They both long for closeness and intimacy, yet their critical spirits are driving a wedge between them.

I can think of at least one more reason we need to avoid criticism: *it saps energy that could be used for the glory of God.* We all know that we should trust God when we are criticized, but we are also very human. We spend an inordinate amount of time thinking and worrying about the unkind things people say to us, and it drains us emotionally. It may even keep us from sleeping at night and then adversely affect our performance the next day. As we well know, criticism is often directed at Christian leaders—preachers, elders, deacons in the church. As mature as they should be, it still causes them pain and produces stress that hinders their ability to minister effectively. They need to learn how to accept criticism, but that does not eliminate the responsibility of Christians who offer it. They will answer to God for the damage they do to God's work.

> **Criticism saps energy that could be used for the glory of God.**

Negative criticism is a poison that kills the enthusiasm of Christian leaders and hinders the progress of God's work. It is a contagious disease that spreads among God's people and can turn a loving community of believers into a battleground. It is a sledgehammer that breaks marriages, homes, and lives into little pieces. That is why Jesus said, "Don't judge." Stop dwelling on the flaws in others, real or perceived.

# The Caution

Notice what Jesus adds to this exhortation not to judge—"so that you will not be judged" (Matt. 7:1). He goes on to explain that warning in the next verse, "For in the way you judge, you will be judged; and by your standard of measure, it will be measured to you." This is what we might call the boomerang principle. We get back what we dish out to others. If we lash out at them with negative criticism, accuse them, scold them, and judge their motives, we are not going to enjoy the results very much. For one thing, they will judge us as being critical and begin to back away from us, the very opposite of what we desire.

Some of us wonder why people are avoiding us and why our circle of friends is diminishing. Could it be that we have been pushing them away by calling attention to their faults with some regularity? They may now be reflecting the same critical attitude back to us, criticizing us for being critical, pushing us away. "Do not judge so that you will not be judged."

When we criticize someone, we are usually insisting on a high standard for him. He is going to use the same standard to judge us that we use to judge him. And God may do the same. The measuring rod we use for others may become God's measuring rod for us. Do you know why that is? Because we usually do the same things we accuse others of doing.

The apostle Paul suggested that principle: "Therefore you have no excuse, everyone of you who passes judgment, for in that which you judge another, you condemn yourself; for you who judge practice the same things" (Rom. 2:1). He was pointing out to the Jews that they were judging Gentiles for the very same things of which they themselves were guilty, but his statement is a penetrating insight into human nature. The things we criticize most in others are usually the very things of which we ourselves are guilty. We don't like those things in ourselves, but we have a tendency to overlook them. Seeing them in others reminds us of them, but instead of dealing with them in our own lives, we focus attention on the same faults in others. As long as we are occupied with *them,* we can avoid changing ourselves. And if we can keep the attention on *them,* they will not be putting pressure on *us* to change.

But it doesn't work. The boomerang principle brings it right back to us. When we wax eloquent about their shortcomings, others can say to us, "Oh, so that's your problem?" Maybe you have heard someone say, "You're nothing but a malicious gossip." In all probability he was someone who consistently put others in a poor light. The people who are the hardest on others usually have the most to hide themselves. For example, the employer who is most severe with the employee who turns out to be a petty thief is probably one who is hiding some major fraud in his own business dealings. The church leader who is most judgmental and punitive with a believer taken in sin may be hiding some sin of his own.

But it will not remain hidden indefinitely. If we do not deal with it, God will have to. "Do not judge so that you will not be judged. For in the way you judge, you will be judged; and by your standard of measure, it shall be measured to you" (Matt. 7:1–2).

## The Contradiction

Christ adds one more thought to this commentary on criticism, and that is the utter contradiction of imperfect people pointing out the imperfections in others. He emphasized the absurdity of it when He said, "Why do you look at the speck in your brother's eye, but do not notice the log that is in your own eye? Or how can you say to your brother, 'Let me take the speck out of your eye,' and behold, the log is in your own eye?" (Matt. 7:3–4). The word *speck* is from the verb that means "to dry up." It refers to any tiny bit of dry material that might blow into the eye, such as a speck of dust, chaff, straw, sawdust, or wool. A beam is exactly that; a heavy plank of wood that would be used as a joist in a building. There is a great lesson for us in these bits and beams.

Can you picture a fellow with a beam sticking out of his eye—a log, a tree trunk, a railroad tie, or a timber? And he is trying to help another fellow get a speck of dust out of his. It is a ridiculous scene. And that is just what the Lord intended. The poor fellow with a speck in his eye would end up with no eye, lumps on his head, and missing teeth, and maybe a great deal more. The point is that we usually have in our own lives much larger editions of the same faults we criticize in others, and people get hurt badly when we try to straighten them out before we straighten ourselves out.

A person who becomes provoked about the faults of others when he has bigger faults of his own is called a hypocrite. "You hypocrite," Jesus said, "first take the log out of your own eye, and then you will see clearly to take the speck out of your brother's eye" (Matt. 7:5). A hypocrite is the woman who says, "If my husband would take his responsibilities more seriously, our marriage could improve," when she is not fulfilling her own responsibilities very faithfully. Or the man who says, "We could be happier if my wife would learn the value of a dollar," when he just spent a bundle on a new shotgun or a new set of golf clubs. A hypocrite is the person who says, "That church isn't interested in soul winning," when it has been years since he has spoken to anyone about Christ. Or, "That church doesn't care about people," when it is nearly impossible to get him to help anybody in need.

Maybe God would have us look at our own lives and engage in some honest self-criticism. Whenever you are tempted to pick at a fault in someone else, ask God instead to show you one of your own. Then ask Him to help you grow in that area. Pray as David prayed, "Search me O God, and know my heart: try me, and know my thoughts: and see if there be any wicked way in me, and lead me in the way everlasting" (Ps. 139:23–24, KJV). That prayer will keep us from being critical of others. And it will bring healing to our lives and to our relationships.

# 3

# MENDING
# NETS

I DON'T LIKE TO ADMIT IT, but I don't always please my wife—and to that fact she readily agrees. I'm human and she's human, and two human beings cannot always please each other. Yet God wants me to please her. There are some things I ought to be doing that I'm not doing. And there are some things I am doing that I shouldn't be doing. What can she do to help me grow? After all, Jesus said she isn't supposed to criticize me.

## What Is the Problem

Every day, Christian counselors listen to long lists of complaints that wives have against their husbands: "He doesn't show me enough love. He doesn't talk to me. He isn't the spiritual leader of the home. He doesn't spend enough time with the children. He doesn't fix things around the house. He doesn't call me when he's going to be late. He squanders money on nonessentials. The husbands have their lists too: "She nags at me. She screams at the kids. She doesn't keep the house clean. She gets irritable over little things. She doesn't take care of her personal appearance. She runs me down to her friends. She isn't interested in me physically."

What are we supposed to do about those things? There are two common but totally destructive alternatives we frequently choose. One is to suppress our feelings and suffer in silence. We all know a sweet, submissive wife who seems to give in to her husband all the time. But she usually finds subtle ways to retaliate that he cannot do anything about (like get a headache at bedtime), and she has her clever schemes to manipulate him into doing what she wants, (like turning on the tears). We probably also know a passive husband who bottles up his resentments and draws into his shell. But he, too, finds little ways to get even (like giving his wife the silent treatment), or he goes out and has an affair. Suppressing our thoughts, feelings, needs, and desires is not the answer.

> **Suppressing our thoughts, feelings, needs, and desires is not the answer.**

On the other end of the spectrum is the person who freely expresses most all of his displeasure. He seldom hesitates to tell people what he thinks of them. He prides himself on his honesty. He tells it like it is! He can wax eloquent about everybody else's faults. But the truth of the matter is, he cares only for himself, and his outspokenness is an attempt to browbeat people into doing what he wants. His so-called honesty is actually thinly veiled anger and hostility. It may succeed in getting others to shape up to his demands, but usually at the cost of hurting them. That is not the edifying love which we are encouraged to express to one another throughout Scripture.

If neither one of these options is acceptable, then what are we supposed to do about the faults of others? There are several passages of Scripture that can help us find an answer to that question. One is Galatians 6:1: "Brethren, if anyone is caught up in any trespass, you who are spiritual, restore such a one in a spirit of gentleness; each one looking to yourself so that you will not be tempted." This verse contains at least five principles for dealing with the faults of other people.

## Be Honest About the Fault

There are such things as trespasses, or faults. In the context, Paul is probably dealing with something into which a person has fallen that will bring reproach on the name of Christ and the testimony of His church. Other believers in the assembly are not simply to ignore it and hope it will disappear. They are to recognize it for what it is—a trespass. The word means "a false step, a blunder, a mistake or an error." It was probably not intentional or premeditated, but it was something that simply caught him off guard. That is the implication of the word "caught."

While Paul's primary reference was probably to sin, the words he chose can apply equally well to all those irritating faults we see in one another. Our friends and spouses are not normally trying to slight us, hurt us, irritate us, embarrass us, or exasperate us on purpose—but they do it nevertheless. They may not realize they are doing it. They may not know how they ought to be acting or what God expects of them. They may not understand that He wants them to be more considerate of and concerned about the wellbeing of others than of themselves. But they are still guilty of a fault. They are falling short of God's standard for their lives.

It is important to note that we are not talking about the little idiosyncrasies that grate on us, the habits that inconvenience us or get on our nerves. We are referring to a fault, something God wants to change. Be honest about it. Recognize it for what it is.

Some of us think it is more spiritual to ignore a fault and quietly put up with it. In reality, we are probably afraid that saying something will lead to an argument. Or we convince ourselves that the other person wouldn't understand what we are trying to say. We think the relationship will be better off if we ignore it. That may be true if we really could ignore it, if we could forget that it ever happened. But usually we don't. We let it eat at us. And our bodies keep score of the hurts we have suffered, and they make us physically ill. Or we let the resentment build and leak out in unexpected ways, corroding our relationships. Or it explodes in anger and unkind words that drive people away from us. Overlooking the matter is not the answer.

> **Some of us think it is more spiritual to ignore a fault and quietly put up with it.**

Furthermore, to allow ourselves to go on being manipulated or victimized by the faults of other people is to condone their selfish and sinful behavior, which will probably be directed at somebody else very soon (if it has not been already). So for the sake of the offender and our relationship with him, as well as for the protection of others who might be hurt, we need to stop making excuses for him and stringing along with him, hoping things will get better. We need to be honest about his faults and confront him. But wait just a minute before you open your mouth. There is a condition you must meet first.

## Prepare Your Own Heart

Paul calls the ones who are qualified to deal with the faults of others, "you who are spiritual (Gal. 6:1)." That does not mean we have to be perfect before we can confront anyone about their faults. No one would ever do it if that were the case. It means that our lives have been dominated by the Holy Spirit of God. We have been walking in the Spirit for awhile. We have given evidence that the Spirit of God has been filling and controlling our lives. The spiritual person is sensitive to God's will, obedient to His Word, motivated by a desire to please Him rather than self, and allowing the Holy Spirit to produce His fruit in his life.

Letting the Spirit of God control our lives is going to help us approach the person in a manner that can bring healing instead of hurt and conflict. If we were honest, we probably would admit that what often motivates us to confront others about their faults is our desire to vent our own anger, irritation, or jealousy, to get even with them for something they have done, to remove some personal inconvenience, to make ourselves look better than they are, or maybe to defend ourselves. Those motives are *not* prompted by the Holy Spirit and, if acted upon, will probably lead to strife. The spiritual person is motivated by love. He wants to build the other person up rather than tear him down. He wants to strengthen the relationship rather than win a point. The "I win, you lose" or "I'm right, you're wrong" approach will make the other person want either to fight or to withdraw—either way, both lose. But when we confront in love in order to build others up, they sense that love and it becomes the spoonful of sugar that helps the medicine go down.

> **The spiritual person is motivated by love.**

Furthermore, the spiritual person also will have earned the right to be heard. His track record reveals that while he is not perfect, he has been growing. He has been letting the Spirit of God shape him up. He is not trying to pick specks out of the eyes of other people when he has logs stuck in his own. He's dealt with his logs. If we want to talk to anybody else about their faults, we need to be working on our own first. We need to prepare our own hearts and lives. But now that we're ready to confront, we must know what the goal is.

## Aim at Restoration

". . . restore such a one . . . ." The word *restore* means "to put in proper condition." Outside the New Testament, the term meant to set broken bones and dislocated limbs. In the Gospels it was used in regard to mending fishing nets (Matt. 4:21; Mark 1:19). The purpose for fishing nets is obviously to catch fish. If the nets are torn, they will not catch many fish; the fish will just swim out through the holes. Torn nets need to be mended.

One of God's purposes for my life is to bring people to Christ and to minister to the needs of others—my wife, my children, and other members of the body of Christ. When my life is torn by faults, I am not going to minister to many needs. I must be mended. And one of the ways that mending can take place is when others confront me about my faults.

The New Testament uses two primary words to describe that confrontation. One is *admonish* or warn. It means literally "to put in mind," but it has the idea of facing someone with his faults and warning him of the consequences of continuing on his present course. Scripture says we are to admonish one another (Rom. 15:14; Col. 3:16). The purpose is obviously not for us to win a point, get one up on another person, prove that we are right and he is wrong, or pin blame on him. The purpose is to bring restoration to that erring one and healing to our relationship. It is to mend the nets. "Admonish the unruly," Paul said to the Thessalonians (1 Thess. 5:14). The purpose of doing so was to restore harmony to the assembly.

> **Gentleness is consideration of others even when they wrong us.**

The second New Testament word for confrontation is *rebuke,* often translated "reprove." It means "to bring to light, expose, set forth; to convict or convince." It refers to telling an offender his fault so that he is convinced of it and wants to correct it. It is the word Jesus used in a helpful passage about confronting an offending brother: "Go and show him his fault in private" (Matt. 18:15).[3] Again, the purpose is not to make us look good and him look bad, but to restore a right relationship between us—to mend the nets. "If he listens to you," Jesus added, "you have won your brother." Suppose you as a Christian wife are fuming at your husband as you ride home from a party. The atmosphere in the car is so thick you can cut it. He flitted from one person to another all evening and left you to fend for yourself. He never so much as spoke to you all evening. You're thinking about what you want to say. "Boy, you really made a fool of yourself tonight. You don't care two cents about me, do you?" Is that really what you want to say? Will those words restore? Hardly! They will let him know what you think, but they accuse and blame. And they will probably be the battle cry for an all-night war. They fail to heed the next principle.

## Maintain the Proper Attitude

Paul explained how we are to restore the believer taken in a fault. It is to be "in a spirit of gentleness." Gentleness is consideration of others even when they wrong us. It enables us to restrain ourselves when our human natures tell us to strike

> **Attacks incite defensiveness, and defensiveness sets the stage for arguments.**

back at them, to hurt them just like they have hurt us. It keeps us from attacking them even when we have the weapons to win. It is strength under control, like a mighty stallion held in check with bit and bridle. This is the attitude one must have to restore a person caught or overtaken in a fault.

The communication experts are consistent with God's Word on this point. They have been telling us for years that we should refrain from making accusations when we confront others. That is the wise way of gentleness. One way we can accomplish that is by focusing on what we are feeling and what we desire instead of on what the other person has done wrong. We do this by making what are called "I" statements rather than "You" statements. Let's try some examples. How do these comments make you feel? "You are so inconsiderate." "You don't really love me, do you?" "You never talk to me." "You sound just like your mother." "You haven't cooked a decent meal for six months." "You think you have to run everything." "You" statements usually constitute an attack on the other person's self worth. Attacks incite defensiveness, and defensiveness sets the stage for arguments.

But nobody can argue with "I" statements. Rather than "You're not thinking about me when you work late," try something like "I feel lonely and rejected when you work late. I very much want you to come home." That explains how you feel and what you want. It doesn't belittle. It doesn't judge motives. Nobody can dispute what you feel or what you want, so there is nothing to argue about. We have confronted what we perceived to be a fault, but we have done it without attacking and accusing. We have done it in gentleness.

> **Gentleness will help us maintain the right tone of voice.**

It might be good to remember that once we have expressed our desire to the other person, we leave the decision to fulfill that desire with him or her. Rather than lock them in the cage of our expectations and try to force them to meet our needs by pressure or manipulation, we trust God to work in their hearts as He chooses. We endeavor to focus on meeting their needs rather than on their meeting ours.

A spirit of gentleness will also help us avoid manipulative questions that put people in traps, especially questions that begin with "Why." "Why are you so lazy?" "Why don't you ever help me?" "Why don't you clean up your messy room?" "Why don't you take better care of your things?" Nobody wants to answer questions like those. To answer is to admit the fault, and they may not be ready for that. Besides, no matter what they say, we'll probably argue and tell them their reasons are not good enough. They can't win and they know it. Questions like that are self-serving and anything but loving and considerate of others. They do not reflect gentleness. Questions are appropriate when our motive is to understand the other person more fully, but not when we use them to trap him.

Gentleness will help us maintain the right tone of voice as well. Our tone can be very incriminating. Some communications experts have estimated that 90 percent of the friction in daily living is caused by the wrong tone of voice. A Christian personnel manager who conducted a pool of employees discovered that they did not resent criticism from their supervisors so much as the way it was given—often maliciously, sarcastically, or harshly. We all prefer to be spoken to kindly and considerately.

Even our children appreciate being spoken to kindly. You can say to your child, "I'd like you to turn the light out when you're finished." Or, you can speak with disgust and sarcasm, "I'd *like you* to turn the *light* out when you're finished!" It is not difficult to determine which one considers the child's feelings and which one is designed to vent your frustration, which one will help build responsibility into his life and which one will build resentment. Whoever it is we are talking to, it might be wise to watch that person's response. If we see antagonism, it would be good to play our words over again in our minds with the same tone and inflections. We will probably detect a lack of gentleness in our tone. That is the time to apologize, then say it again, gently.

Gentleness will also encourage us to use what some have called "the sandwich principle"—that is, sandwiching the suggestion between layers of praise. Christ Jesus did that when He confronted the church at Ephesus. First He said He knew their toil and perseverance (Rev. 2:2–3). That is commendation Then He faced them with leaving their primary love (Rev. 2:4–5). That is confrontation. Finally He acknowledged that they did hate the deeds of the Nicolaitans (Rev. 2:6) That is commendation again.

That is a good model to follow. When we build a positive, accepting, approving relationship with people, one saturated with praise and commendation, they can respond more easily to our confrontation without feeling threatened or rejected. It is the considerate thing to do. It is the spirit of gentleness, and it mends nets rather than tears them to shreds. But Paul feels constrained to add one more thought to this formula in Galatians 6:1 for dealing with the faults of others.

## Acknowledge Your Own Weakness

You should approach them "each one looking to yourself, so that you too will not be tempted." There is no way we can properly confront others with an air of superiority. Biblical confrontation is just one sinner sharing with another something that might make them both better people and make their relationship with each other stronger and more satisfying. Suggestions are easier to take from someone who lets you know he has the same weaknesses you have.

But for the grace of God, we would be doing the same thing he is doing. In fact, we probably have. And we very well may again. Remembering that will keep us from a vindictive, condemning, and holier-than-thou attitude, and will help us maintain a gentle, kind and calm tone. Then the nets will be mended, and together we will fulfill God's purposes for our lives—ministering to each other's needs, contributing to each other's lives, and building each other up for the glory of God.

# 4

# THE CUTTING
# EDGE

WOULDN'T IT BE WONDERFUL if nobody ever criticized us, never picked at our faults, never pointed out our weaknesses, or reminded us of our mistakes? Most of us would be delighted to live our lives without negative criticism. But we won't! We're not perfect, and somewhere along the way, somebody is going to point that out to us.

Moses was a man who took his share of criticism. He was just trying to do what God wanted him to do, yet people kept criticizing him. Six separate occasions are recorded in Scripture when the Israelites murmured or grumbled against him. That word *murmur* means "to express resentment, dissatisfaction, anger, and complaint by grumbling in half-muted tones of hostile opposition . . ."4 In other words, it means to criticize. I do not know anybody in Scripture except the Lord Jesus who felt the sharp edge of cutting criticism more keenly than Moses. Moses was not perfect in the way he handled it, but he surely did better than most of us would do, and we can learn some lessons from his example.

What we need is a plan, a procedure carefully thought out beforehand which we can call to mind readily and put into action quickly when the critic strikes. Maybe the word PLAN itself can be the key to remembering four helpful principles illustrated from the life of Moses:

P—Pray

L—Listen and learn

A—Answer positively

N—Note the critic's needs

## Pray

What is your first reaction when it becomes obvious that the person talking to you is actually finding fault? If you are a normal human being, your reaction is the same as mine—you defend yourself. It is just as natural as closing your eye when someone accidentally pokes his finger in it. Criticism hurts; it cuts our spirits and we automatically recoil from it.

Moses did not like it any more than we do, but somehow he learned to react differently. Instead of defending himself, he developed the habit of turning to God in prayer. It seems to have been an automatic response with him. We see it first at Marah. The children of Israel had crossed the Red Sea and had sung a jubilant song of redemption. Then we read, "And when they came to Marah, they could not drink the waters of Marah, for they were bitter; therefore it was named Marah. So the people grumbled at Moses, saying, 'What shall we drink?'" (Ex. 15:23–24). I probably would have responded, "Hey, don't blame me. I didn't make the water bitter. At least you're not getting beat up with Egyptian whips. Count your blessings." Moses didn't do that. Instead we read, "He cried out to the LORD . . ." (Ex. 15:25). His mind was on the Lord, so his immediate response was to turn to Him in prayer.

We see that same pattern repeated over and over in Moses' life. On later occasions he actually fell on his face before God in an attitude of prayer (cf. Num. 14:5; 16:4). He humbly committed himself to the Lord. He recognized that when he was trying to do the will of God, and people criticized him for it, it was God's problem, not his. So he turned to God for wisdom.

> **Criticism hurts; it cuts our spirits and we automatically recoil from it.**

Moses even *said* it was God's problem the next time he was criticized—in the Wilderness of Sin (no intended connection of the place name with the Israelites' behavior). This time the people scolded him because they had no food: ". . . For you have brought us out into this wilderness to kill this whole assembly with hunger" (Ex. 16:3). Ouch! That hurts. What a caustic and cutting thing to say, and they knew it was blatantly false when they said it. We probably would have told them how ridiculous their accusation was and how much we had done for them. But Moses just committed it to the Lord. ". . . For the LORD hears your grumblings which you grumble against Him. And what are we? Your grumblings are not against us but against the LORD" (Ex. 16:8). He was saying basically, "We are nobody. Your complaint is not with us. It is with God. He controls the circumstances."

It would be good for us to commit the situation to the Lord and go directly to Him in prayer when a barrage of criticism is unleashed against us, just as Moses did. We can believe that He is in control of what is happening—even the indignity that we may be suffering at that moment—and we can commit it to Him in prayer. We can ask Him to help us listen patiently, to be aware of what He wants us to learn, to control our anger, to respond positively, and to be sensitive to the needs of the critic. We can even pray that God will bless the critic. Jesus told us to do that. "But I say to you, love your enemies, bless those who curse you . . . and pray for those who spitefully use you and persecute you" (Matt. 5:44, KJV).

Moses actually did that! It was at Kadesh Barnea after the ten spies brought back a discouraging report that the criticism started again. "And all the sons of Israel complained against Moses and Aaron; and the whole congregation said to them, 'Would that we had died in the land of Egypt! Or if only we had died in this wilderness!'" (Num. 14:2). They even threatened to fire Moses, choose a new captain, and return to Egypt. This time God became exasperated with them. He wanted to exterminate the whole community and make of Moses a greater and mightier nation. But Moses prayed, "Pardon, I pray, the iniquity of this people according to the greatness of Your lovingkindness, just as You also have forgiven this people, from Egypt even until now" (Num. 14:19). And God pardoned them. What an example for us!

There was another instance of Moses praying for his critics, and this time they were members of his own family. Aaron and Miriam criticized Moses for taking a Cushite wife and for assuming too much authority on himself. God struck Miriam with leprosy for her unsubmissive spirit. A lesser man may have said something like, "It serves you right. Now we all know who's in charge here." But not Moses. He turned to the Lord and prayed for her healing (Numbers 12). That kind of attitude can bring harmony and strength to our relationships, even with critical people.

**We need to learn to keep our minds on the Lord.**

We need to learn to keep our minds on the Lord. Then they will be there, fixed on Him, when critics start using "the cutting edge" on us. Our first reaction will be to talk to Him rather then to defend ourselves. And that in itself may defuse a potentially explosive situation. The first thing we need to do, and the most important of all, is pray!

## Listen and Learn

It isn't easy to listen when somebody is cutting us to shreds with words, or even when they are giving us a mild and much-needed rebuke. Before their first few sentences are out, most of us are thinking how wrong they are about us and what good reasons we had for doing what we are being criticized for doing. We are formulating our reply already before they are finished saying what they want to say, and we even may interrupt them to justify ourselves (which, by the way, is not a very good idea). Solomon said, "He who gives an answer before he hears, it is folly and shame to him" (Prov. 18:13).

> **"He who gives an answer before he hears, it is folly and shame to him."**

The godly critic probably has thought about the problem for some time. He knows it would be unpleasant to tell us about it, but he cares enough about us to endure the unpleasantness in order to help us. He knows he may arouse our hostility, but he cares enough about us to take that chance. That is really a compliment. Even if he is guilty of an emotional outburst, he probably has mulled it over in his mind for awhile before speaking. So listen and learn! As Solomon reminded us, "Faithful are the wounds of a friend" (Prov. 27:6).

Moses listened and learned. When his father-in-law criticized the way he was judging the people and suggested an alternative, we read, "So Moses listened to his father-in-law, and did all that he had said" (Ex. 18:24). We can do the same. Let the critic finish. Interruptions may keep us from ever hearing what is on his heart. Take notes on what he says. When he seems to be finished, be sure he has said everything he wants to say before you answer. You could say, "Is there anything else you'd like to share with me?" Or, "I wasn't aware of that. Would you tell me why you feel that way?" Communicate genuinely and sincerely that you are interested in hearing what he has to say.

It is important to realize that this experience is not by accident, unpleasant though it may be. View it as a learning opportunity. It may be God's way of getting our attention and showing us something about ourselves we have not been willing to acknowledge—some offensive attitude or habit that may be causing somebody to stumble.

Others see things in us we cannot see ourselves. Our own family members are particularly expert at seeing our faults. And as difficult as it may be to hear it from them, listen and learn. Compliments make us happy, but criticism can help us grow.

**Listen and learn!**

Unfortunately, some of us would rather be destroyed by flattery than strengthened by criticism. But if people as great and godly as Moses could learn and grow through criticism, we surely can too.

## Answer Positively

Up until now we have been talking about what takes place in our own souls, our inner thoughts and attitudes—prayer, a willingness to listen and a desire to learn. But now it is time to respond, and God would have us answer positively. That means, first of all, that we will answer calmly and quietly As a well-known proverb puts it, "A gentle answer turns away wrath" (Prov. 15:1). If the critic is angry and hostile, a gentle spirit can be used of God to calm him down and make the whole discussion more profitable. An angry, indignant reply is negative; it fuels the fire and makes any profitable communication impossible. A gentle response is positive.

We are reminded of Moses' meek and gentle spirit in one of the most provocative attacks he suffered, that of his brother and sister, Aaron and Miriam. Immediately after their angry, self-centered accusations, and before we learn of God's righteous discipline, the Holy Spirit saw fit to insert these insightful words: "Now the man Moses was very humble, more than any man who was on the face of the earth" (Num. 12:3). So follow Moses' example. Maintain a gentle and humble spirit.

A second element in a positive response is to be sure you understand what the critic is saying. Much hard feeling has lingered among believers because people have assumed they understood what others were saying when they really did not. Sometimes words are poorly chosen, or in the heat of anger things are exaggerated or overstated. It might be good to say something like, "What I hear you saying is _____. Am I understanding you correctly?" Give him opportunity to clarify. Repeating it a second time helps him say it more calmly and with less animosity. People who handle complaints over the telephone are taught to politely ask the customer to repeat his complaint. Invariably it is clearer and calmer the second time around. Sincerely requesting clarification is a positive way to answer.

**A gentle response is positive.**

Now we understand what is bothering the critic about us, and we must do some honest, objective self evaluation. The sovereign God of the universe has allowed some human being to express what he perceives to be a fault in us. We cannot take that lightly. A third factor in a positive reply is to find the truth in what he says and immediately agree with everything we can possibly agree with. Jesus said, "Agree with thine adversary quickly" (Matt. 5:25, KJV). Agreeing with the critic will tend to blunt the sharpness of his spirit.

Most of us are reluctant to admit our failures. We consider what we do and say as so closely tied to what we are that to admit we were wrong is to give up some of our self worth. We believe people will think less of us. We want to sweep it under the carpet and forget about it. It is painful to admit it. But the consequences of admitting it are so refreshing, we cannot afford not to. Nothing can restore harmony and healing to strained relationships as effectively as admitting we were wrong and then correcting it. If there is just a grain of truth in it, admit it. The critic says, "You did a terrible job!" You can reply, "I know I could have done it better."

The critic says, "You think of nobody but yourself." You can reply, "I admit that I have a tendency to be self-centered." Those are positive answers that defuse the explosiveness of their attacks.

Sometimes we honestly cannot see that the criticism is valid right there on the spot. Rather than defend ourselves, it might be better to say, "I appreciate you calling that to my attention. I'll need some time to think about it." Then do just that. Give it serious thought. Ask God to show you the elements of truth in it. Then go back and acknowledge them to the person who leveled the criticism. Seldom will any of us be so perfect that we cannot find any truth at all in the criticism people level against us. It's there! Find it, and admit it.

> **Agreeing with the critic will tend to blunt the sharpness of his spirit.**

A fourth positive response would be to ask for the critic's help in finding a solution to the problem or a way of correcting the weakness. Ask, "What do you think I should do?" That can melt away the barriers and bring us together instead of pitting us against one another as arguing or defending ourselves will do. Discovering a mutually agreeable course of action becomes the common goal that helps us overcome our differences.

There may be times when a criticism is absolutely invalid. It is based on hearsay, secondhand opinion, false assumptions, or imagined slights. We have taken the time to think about it, to apply the Word of God to our lives, and to ask God to show us the elements of truth in it. But we still consider it to be false. We now have two choices. We can go back and say something like, "You're wrong, and let me tell you something, buddy. You're not so great yourself." But counter-accusations will only escalate the hostility. It would be much more positive and helpful to explain lovingly, graciously, kindly, and without resentment or vindictiveness that we have examined our hearts before God and cannot honestly admit to their evaluation. We might add, "I'm sorry you feel as you do, but I hope it won't affect our relationship." Then we can pray that God will help them to see the truth and bring us together.

## Note the Critic's Needs

**God wants us to reach out in love.**

Sometimes the people who criticize us have far deeper problems than what they are accusing us of having. Their hostility may actually be a smokescreen to hide their own faults, or a muted cry for help. It may stem from their own insecurity, or the fact that they do not like themselves very much. By God's grace, we can see past the cutting criticism to the people themselves. It does not do them one bit of good for us to prove that we are right and they are wrong. What accomplishes the greatest good is showing them forgiveness, patience, understanding, and acceptance. God wants us to reach out in love to minister to their needs.

There is a beautiful example of that in Moses' experience. When Korah and over 250 other high-ranking princes in Israel criticized Moses for usurping too much authority, God took their lives in an awesome display of divine discipline (Num. 16:1–40). That was when the rest of the nation started criticizing him again. "But on the next day all the congregation of the sons of Israel grumbled against Moses and Aaron, saying, 'You are the ones who have caused the death of the LORD's people.'" (Num. 16:41). God has just about had it with them. "And the LORD spoke to Moses, saying, 'Get away from among this congregation, that I may consume them instantly'" (Num. 16:44–45). I would think Moses might have said, "Go get 'em, Lord." That's probably what I would have done. Instead, he instructed Aaron to hurry to the tabernacle and offer a sacrifice of atonement for them, and the Scripture records that the plague was checked (Num. 16:48). That is a man who looks past the criticism to the people and their needs, then reaches out in love to minister to those needs.

When someone criticizes us, it would be good to ask ourselves, "What is happening in his life to make him this critical? What hurts is he feeling? What needs are not being met? How can I show him that I care about him?" That is not easy to do when someone is cutting us to pieces with words. It takes grace. But isn't that what God has promised? He is the God of all grace (1 Peter 5:10). If we become channels of God's grace, He can use us to make other lives vastly more effective in His service.

Satan can use criticism to discourage us and distract us from doing the will of God. If every time we try to do something, somebody shoots us out of the saddle, eventually we may be tempted to say, "That's enough. I'll just hang up my spurs." Don't do it. Reexamine your direction. If God has led you, then keep moving ahead. Don't let petty criticism from little people dissuade you from your commitment.

I read the story of a small-town judge who was frequently ridiculed by an egotistical lawyer. When asked why he didn't rebuke him, the judge said, "In our town there is a widow who has a dog. Whenever the moon shines, the dog goes outside and barks all night." Then he began talking about something else. Someone said, "But, Judge, what about the dog and the moon?" "Oh," he replied, "the moon just keeps right on shining."

If we are wrong, we have no business defending ourselves. God wants us to be open to correction. But if we are right, we have no need to defend ourselves. We can just keep on shining, keep on doing the will of God with greater dependence on Him. The cutting edge of criticism will not hurt us when we let it drive us to God in greater trust. Instead, it will keep us serving Him with renewed enthusiasm, renewed determination, and renewed power from on high. Will you memorize the PLAN we have discussed? Will you be alert to the criticism directed toward you and apply the principles you have learned?

**P—Pray**
**L—Listen and learn**
**A—Answer positively**
**N—Note the critic's needs**

# 5

# A MATTER OF
# LIFE AND DEATH

**D**ID YOU KNOW that you carry a lethal weapon with you wher-ever you go? And it would be impossible for anyone to make you check it at the door, because it is attached to your body. The Spirit of God led Solomon to write, "Death and life are in the power of the tongue" (Prov. 18:21). That is an amazing state-ment—and truer than we care to think. James said the tongue is full of deadly poison (James 3:8). A frightening thought!

The story of what happened to a family in a small North Dakota community illustrates this truth. The mother had not been well since the birth of her second baby, but everyone knew she did all she could to create an atmosphere of love in the home. The neighbors could see the father being met at the door each evening with hugs and kisses from his wife and two small children. In summer when the windows were open, they could hear the

> **Death and life are in the power of the tongue.**

laughter and joyous fun coming from inside the house.

Then one day a village gossip whispered that the man was being unfaithful to his wife, a story completely without basis. It was passed on by others, and eventually came to his wife's ears. It was more than she could bear. One evening when her husband came home, no one met him at the door. There was a deathly silence in the air. His wife had taken her own life and those of her two children. He was overcome with grief. His innocence was proven to all, but the gossip's tongue had already done its work. Death and life are in the power of the tongue. It is full of deadly poison.

Most of us who know the Lord want our conversations to honor Him. We want our communication habits to promote love and unity in the body of Christ. But too often we use our built-in weapons system to accomplish the very opposite. Then we wonder why there is so much conflict among God's people. A study of Scripture may help us find the antidote for the poison of gossip.

## The Cause for Gossip

While the word *gossip* is not prominent in the Bible, the idea is sprinkled throughout its pages. It mentions talebearers, people who whisper derogatory information about others. It mentions backbiters, people who talk about faults of others behind their backs. It mentions slanderers, people who speak against others, often with a desire to do them harm. It talks about speaking evil of people or maligning them. We can sum it all up with one word: gossip. It is an ugly word—so ugly, hardly anyone will ever admit to doing it: they have valid concerns; they want to share a matter for prayer; but they never *gossip!*

> **Gossip is an ugly word.**

We have studied a critical spirit, that is, preoccupation with the faults of others. Gossip is talking about those faults to people who cannot do anything about them, people who are neither a part of the problem nor a part of the solution. And talking about them to others is gossip, whether it is rumor or fact, true or false. God says, "Do not speak against one another, brethren" (James 4:11). That injunction does not say anything about whether it is true or false. It is evidently unacceptable to speak against other believers even if the story is true.

It is even wrong to do it in the form of a prayer request: "Pray for John—he's deep in debt." Or in speaking to God publicly, we say, "Father, please deal with John. You

> **Gossip seems to be one of the Christian's favorite pastimes.**

know he can't control his spending habits." It is wrong to spread accounts of the sins of other people, to put them in a bad light, to say things that will cause other people to dislike them, disrespect them, or distrust them. Gossip is listed alongside the vilest sins imaginable. Listen to Paul's lineup of gross sinners:

"Being filled with all unrighteousness, wickedness, greed, malice; full of envy, murder, strife, deceit, malice; they are gossips, slanderers, haters of God, insolent, arrogant, boastful, inventors of evil, disobedient to parents, without understanding, untrustworthy, unloving, unmerciful" (Rom. 1:29–30). Yet gossip seems to be another one of the Christian's favorite pastimes. Why?

Most of us want others to think well of us. If we were honest, we would admit that a good bit of our thought-life is occupied with our acceptance level: "Do they know who I am? Do they like me? Do they respect me? Do they think I know what I'm talking about? Do they think I'm attractive? Do they like what I'm wearing? Do they want to be with me?" The lower our self esteem is, the more we worry about things like that, but all of us give some thought to them. That, however, is why we gossip.

We want to make ourselves look better and gain greater acceptance. If we have confidential information others do not have, it makes us appear important, knowledgeable, and superior. People will listen to us. If we fear somebody else excels us in some way, cutting them down helps us excuse our failure to achieve what they have achieved. If we are jealous of the attention or acclaim they get, pointing out their faults makes us look a little better by comparison. If somebody has injured us, putting them in a bad light seems to us to be a fair way of retaliating, balancing the scales and restoring some of our self esteem. It can also be an effective way of winning people to our side in the conflict. We seem to think that having more people on our side gives us greater worth. It would help us more, though, if we realized that God loves us as we are, that He has accepted us if we are now "in Christ" and granted us each a place in the body of Christ with a significant role to fill. We don't need to put others in bad light to establish our own value.

> **We don't need to put others in bad light to establish our own value.**

There are other reasons we gossip. For one thing, we may have had a poor example. We grew up hearing our parents gossip and so were led to believe it was an acceptable part of life. Another possibility is that we have not developed our minds to the extent that we have anything else to talk about but people. Somebody has suggested that folks with great minds talk about ideas, folks with average minds talk about events, and folks with small minds talk about other people. It would help to develop our minds.

The apostle Paul suggested that we may gossip because we do not have anything better to do. He talks about young widows who "learn to be idle, as they go around from house to house; and not merely idle, but also gossips and busybodies, talking about things not proper to mention" (1 Tim. 5:13). Gossip here is foolish talk, especially talk that incriminates others. Their gossip is tied both to their idleness and to their tendency to be busybodies, that is, meddling in the affairs of other people. If they invested their time and energies into spiritually profitable activities such as visiting rest homes, ministering to shut-ins, or caring for children, they would not have time to chatter about other people. But the cause for gossip is not nearly as important as the damage it does.

> **The cause for gossip is not nearly as important as the damage it does.**

## The Consequences of Gossip

The book of Proverbs is like a textbook on the tongue, and it mentions several damaging effects of gossip. The first is that it separates friends. "A perverse man spreads strife, and a slanderer separates intimate friends" (Prov. 16:28). "He who conceals a transgression seeks love, but he who repeats a matter separates intimate friends" (Prov. 17:9). Sometimes gossip is done purposely and maliciously by a jealous person who resents the friends someone else has. If he can dig up any trace of disreputable information, he will use it to drive a wedge between friends so he can try to move into the gap. He finds that to be easier than winning friends by showing genuine, unselfish kindness to others. "I don't mean to be talking about her, but . . ." "I don't want you to think I'm gossiping, but . . ." And in goes the knife!

On the other hand, there may be no malicious intent. It is just idle talk, or an effort to appear on the "inside." But the result is just the same. You may have heard about the conversation where Ellen says, "Suzie told me you told her the secret that I told you not to tell her." Jane answers, "Why that blabbermouth! I told her not to tell you I told her." So Ellen replies, "Well, I told her I wouldn't tell you she told me, so don't tell her I did." That friendship is doomed. Friends have to be able to trust each other. "He who goes about as a talebearer reveals secrets, but he who is trustworthy conceals a matter" (Prov. 11:13).

We alienate our own closest friends by gossip. They begin to suspect that if we talk about others to them, we will also talk about them to others, so they hesitate to share their souls with us. And if we do talk about them, you can be sure it will get back to them, usually exaggerated by a few degrees. And no matter how much we protest that we did not say exactly that, the friendship could be irreparably damaged. "Death and life are in the power of the tongue, and those who love it [that is, love to use their tongues] will eat its fruit" (Prov. 18:21). If we use the tongue for good, we will reap good from it. If we use it to cast shadows, those shadows will eventually fall on us.

> **We alienate our own closest friends by gossip.**

Another consequence of gossip is that it wounds people. "The words of a whisperer are like dainty morsels, and they go down into the innermost parts of the body" (Prov. 18:8). How do you feel when you find out that people have been talking about you unfavorably? They may have enjoyed it as one would enjoy a dainty morsel, but it hurts you, doesn't it? And the hurt reaches down to your innermost being. While we know the Lord wants us to forgive them, we usually stew on it, worry over it, fret about it, feel sorry for ourselves, and get angry with them. Sometimes it begins to affect our ability to function properly. And it may take a long time to heal. Think about that the next time you are tempted to share some juicy tidbit about someone. Would you want that told about you, even if it were true?

Gossip not only wounds—it also destroys. I have a pastor friend, in his late sixties, who put his arm innocently on the shoulder of a single female missionary who had just returned from the field. A few people in the congregation saw him and nearly ended his ministry. Another gracious, godly, and extremely capable pastor in my acquaintance was forced to resign his pastorate because an associate began to sow seeds of suspicion and doubt about his abilities, even making insinuations about his sanity. Servants of the Lord have been destroyed by other men in the ministry who thought they knew what their colleagues believed, but who misrepresented it publicly and attacked them personally. How that must grieve the heart of God!

Gossip likewise instigates anger. "The north wind brings forth rain, and a backbiting tongue, an angry countenance" (Prov. 25:23). Some of the angriest people I have ever talked to have been the victims of vicious gossip. They were furious. The resentment they have built up as a result of the anger is sin, and they need to resolve it. But the person with the runaway tongue will still answer for his disobedience to God's Word.

**Gossip not only wounds—it also destroys.**

Did you ever turn a garden hose on with the nozzle partially open? It flops around, bangs into things and soaks everyone nearby. Those people are not very happy with you, are they? A flopping tongue, spraying poison of gossip, has even worse consequences. Husbands and wives have made their family and friends furious with their spouses by talking about faults. Some who have heard the dirt have never been able to forget it, resulting in their inability to accept the one about whom the gossip has been told. The anger lives on.

That leads to the final consequence of gossip we want to mention. Gossip causes contention and strife. "For lack of wood the fire goes out, and where there is no whisperer, contention quiets down" (Prov. 26:20). We all have known of local churches which were wracked with strife. But there never has been one where the strife would not disappear if people would stop gossiping. "Do you know what he said? Do you know what she did? I'll tell you what I think he's after. If he would just do his job, everything would be all right. Do you know what that committee is up to now?" And so on. Foolish talk. But it is like wood on the fire. It gets other people stirred up, and they get other people stirred up, and what started out as a spark turns into a raging fire.

James tells us where the original spark comes from. He said it "is set on fire by hell" (James 3:6). Satan loves it. Gossip is his game. The name *devil* means "slanderer," and he is called "the accuser of our brethren" (Rev. 12:10). But God hates it. He says the person who spreads strife among brothers is an abomination to Him (Prov. 6:16–19).

Well, after examining what God says about gossip, what are we going to do about it?

## The Cure for Gossip

The first suggestion for eliminating gossip from our conversations is to obey the command of Christ and confront others directly. "And if your brother sins, go and show him his fault in private; if he listens to you, you have won your brother" (Matt. 18:15). God

**Gossip causes contention and strife.**

wants us to confront those who wrong us. If somebody does something to offend us, slight us, wrong us, take advantage of us, or fail us in some way, or if we are aware of a serious sin which somebody has committed, we are to talk to that person about it—nobody else, just him alone! If it is some petty little thing, maybe we should just forgive him and forget about it. But if it is important enough to talk to anybody else about, we must talk to him about it first. And if it is not important enough to talk to him, then there is no need ever to mention it to anyone else.

I have asked people on occasion if they have confronted the person who offended them and their answer has been, "Yes, and it didn't do any good." So now they feel justified in telling others. But there is a second step prescribed by our Lord, and it is not to spread the word among our friends. "But if he does not listen to you, take one or two more with you, so that by the mouth of two or three witnesses every fact may be confirmed" (v.16). Have you done that?

Then there is another step. "If he refuses to listen to them, tell it to the church; and if he refuses to listen even to the church, let him be to you as a Gentile and a tax collector" (v. 17). Have you done that? Nowhere in this procedure does it say, "Okay, now you can go tell all your friends." That is never a biblical option! And consistent biblical attempts to resolve the problem will help eliminate the temptation to talk about it to others.

The second suggestion for eliminating gossip is simply to refuse to listen to it. "He who goes about as a slanderer reveals secrets, therefore do not associate with a gossip" (Prov. 20:19). If all of us would follow that advice, the gossips would have nobody to infect with their venom. When Mrs. Motormouth calls a friend at church and starts to unload her dirt about Gracie Gadabout, her friend should say, "It would be good if you talked to Gracie about that. I don't feel comfortable with the information." She will probably call another friend and try again, but if she gets the same response four or five times, she will either clean up her speech habits or look for a new church. In either case, that church will be spared the poison of her gossiping tongue.

It is difficult not to listen when somebody starts giving us some high level, top-secret information. It makes us feel important to think that they would choose to tell us. Our old sin natures prompt us to take it in and store it up so we can use it someday to enhance our own image. But the listener is just as guilty as the gossiper. People talk because other people listen. If nobody listened, gossip would cease.

A third suggestion for overcoming gossip is to be more open about our own weaknesses. We like to keep our problems under cover for the sake of our image. If we're not getting along with our spouse, or one of the children ran away from home, or we're having difficulties on the job, we don't want anyone to know in case it destroys our reputation as a Christian. But our secrecy not only deprives us of the healing which the rest of the Body can minister to us; it also provides grist for the rumor mill. If we openly shared those problems and personally solicited the prayer

> One suggestion for overcoming gossip is to be more open about our own weaknesses.

support of other believers, we would be helped immensely, and the mystery on which the gossip feeds would be done away. There is no reason to gossip if everyone knows about it already.

God wants *me* to be open about *my* weaknesses, and *you* to be open about *your* weaknesses. But that is where it stops. He doesn't want me to be open about yours, nor you to be open about mine. Openness itself can turn to gossip when we misuse it. You all have heard of the three preachers who were out in a boat together fishing. They decided to get honest with each other about their secret sins. The first preacher said he liked to gamble when he got away from home. The second said he took a little drink of liquor when no one was looking. "What's yours?" they asked the third. "Mine's gossip," he answered, "and I can't wait to get back to shore!" That is not the kind of openness we are talking about. Let each of us be honest about our own shortcomings.

A fourth suggestion is to learn to love. We learn that primarily by observing God's love for us (cf. 1 John 4:19). And when we truly learn it, we will not gossip any more. "Hatred stirs up strife, but love covers all transgressions" (Prov. 10:12). That idea was borrowed by Peter who said, "Above all, keep fervent in your love for one another, because love covers a multitude of sins" (1 Peter 4:8). The worst thing about gossip is that it is totally unloving. We are showing no loving consideration whatsoever for the person we talk about in a derogatory manner. We are tearing him down before others, whereas love builds him up (cf. 1 Cor. 8:1).

Before we open our mouths it might be good to ask, "Will this build respect for the person I am about to mention? Will it build trust? Will it build love?" If not, it would be better to leave it unsaid. There are many things I have said through the years that I wish I could take back, but it is too late! Thoughtless, loveless words can never be reclaimed. Learn to love!

There is one more suggestion, the most obvious and most important, yet probably the least used. Ask the Lord to help you guard your tongue. The psalmist did. "Let the words of my mouth and the meditation of my heart be acceptable in Your sight, O LORD, my rock and my Redeemer" (Ps. 19:14). "Set a guard, O LORD, over my mouth; Keep watch over the door of my lips" (Ps. 141:3). God loves to help people who humbly admit their need and ask Him for help. Will you try it? He will help you conquer the gossip habit.

**Thoughtless, loveless words can never be reclaimed.**

# 6

# "BE HONEST
WITH ME"

MOST CHRISTIANS WANT TO GET ALONG well with the significant people in our lives—our families, friends, neighbors, fellow workers, and fellow believers. We would like to know there are good feelings between us, to enjoy a pleasant sense of oneness and togetherness.

Did you know that God wants exactly the same thing for us? It is expressed in Paul's letter to the Ephesians. In the first three chapters Paul shows us how much God loves us and what He has done for us, particularly how He united us together in one Body. Then Paul begins the second half of the book by saying, "Therefore, I, the prisoner of the Lord, implore you to walk in a manner worthy of the calling with which you have been called, with all humility and gentleness, with patience, showing tolerance to one another in love, being diligent to preserve the unity of the Spirit in the bond of peace. There is one body and one Spirit, just as also you were called in one hope of your calling; one Lord, one faith, one baptism, one God and Father of all who is over all and through all and in all" (Eph. 4:1–6). Do you get the point? There is a built-in oneness in the Christian faith that can now be expressed in our relationships with one another. We should be able to get along with each other in love and peace and enjoy a sense of togetherness because we are one in Christ.

## How Can We Learn to Get Along?

It's strange, isn't it? We know what God wants, and we know that the structure for it exists, yet we have so much difficulty practicing it. Instead, we have disagreements and hard feelings. We see husbands and wives fussing with each other, parents and children quarreling, Christian neighbors feuding, church members on the outs with one another. How can we change that? How can we learn to get along with each other?

The fourth chapter of Ephesians, probably more than any other in the New Testament, helps us answer that question. For one thing, God gives us spiritual gifts by which we can minister to one another and help one another (vv. 1:1–12). That will bring us to unity and Christlikeness (v. 13), which enables us to be built up in love (v. 16).

> **We should be able to get along with each other because we are one in Christ.**

But that is not the entire answer. As the chapter progresses, it becomes increasingly clear that in order to get along with each other we will need to make some changes in our lives. We will need to live differently from the way unbelievers live, from the way we used to live before we knew Christ (v. 17). The provision has been made. When Christ died on the cross He condemned the old nature which is dominated by sin and self. He removed its authority over us (v. 22), and He gave us a new nature which is patterned after His own (v. 24).

With that provision, we now have the potential for making the changes that will help us get along with one another. But there are still some things we must do in order to make this potential real in our daily experience. For one thing, we will need to renew our minds (v. 23), that is, feed into our minds God's perspective on life generally. That will strengthen the control of our new natures over us. But we also will need to put aside the acts of our sinful nature consciously and choose instead to let our new Spirit-empowered nature act in each situation we face. We will need to reject the old way of acting and choose to let the Spirit of God act through us as He Himself wishes in each situation. We will need to put off the old and put on the new in each new circumstance we face.

Paul lists some of the areas in which we will need to do that by a series of contrasts—first the negative, then the positive. Put off lying and speak the truth (v. 25). Stop stealing and do an honest day's work (v. 28). Do not speak corrupt words, but speak edifying words (v. 29). Put away anger, and be kind (vv. 31–32). It is interesting to note how many of these areas have to do with our speech. The key to getting along with each other is how we use our mouths. And right at the top of the list is *truthfulness*. If we want harmony in our relationships, we will need to tell the truth. "Therefore, laying aside falsehood, speak truth each one of you with his neighbor, for we are members of one another" (v. 25).

> **We need to feed into our minds God's perspective on life generally.**

## The Meaning of the Command

To lay aside falsehood is to stop making any statements that are untrue, and stop acting in any way that deceives or leaves a false impression. There are any number of ways we can dabble in falsehood. For one thing, we can simply say what we know to be untrue.

Let me tell you about Henry, a man who struggles with his self image. He longs to be viewed as a strong, wise, capable individual who has it all together, but he suspects that people view him as a loser. Rather than become all he can be by God's power, and be happy with himself in that capacity, he finds it easier to present himself to be more than he is. He tells his wife how pleased the boss is with his work, when in reality he is on the verge of being fired. When he gets fired, he insists that he quit, and that he had to do it because his working conditions were so bad. Then he will keep telling his wife that he has a good prospect for a new job which is sure to materialize next week, when there really are no prospects at all. He tells his friends about the fantastic business deals he has in the making, but it is all fabricated to make him look better than he suspects he is.

That is the way many unbelievers live. It is part of their sinful natures. They inherit it from their father Satan who Jesus said is a liar and the father of lies (John 8:44). And those who go on habitually lying are indicating that they are his children. God is the God of truth, and those who have His nature speak the truth. Lying lips are an abomination to Him (Prov. 12:22), and He hates a lying tongue (Prov. 6:16–19).

> **God is the God of truth, and lying lips are an abomination to Him.**

That is not to say that a true Christian can never lie. Ananias and Sapphira were true Christians, but they wanted to appear better than they actually were. They wanted people to think that they were giving to the church the entire proceeds from the sale of their land. They didn't actually say that; they just let people believe it. We can lie by silence too, but it is still lying. Peter said, "Ananias, why has Satan filled your heart to lie to the Holy Spirit?" (Acts 5:3). And we get an idea of how seriously God views the intent to deceive because He took both Ananias and his wife in death.

There are other ways we distort the truth. One is to exaggerate. Fishermen are not the only ones who do that, you know. Most of us take our turn. If we had any part in planning or running a meeting, we may find it advantageous to stretch the attendance figures a little. That makes us look good. We may exaggerate our contribution to any successful venture because we want people to think we are important. In trying to make a point, we may say, "A lot of people have told me . . .," when in reality only one person said it, and maybe it was our husband or wife.

**Exaggeration distorts the truth.**

Another way we shade the truth is to tell only what suits our purpose. If we are involved in a confrontation with someone, we may find it to our advantage to slant the facts slightly to favor our own point of view or tell only part of the story. A wife said to her husband, "The counselor said this never would have happened if you had done what you were supposed to do." But she conveniently forgot to mention what the counselor told her she did to agitate the situation.

One of our most common forms of lying as believers involves the way we cover up the shortcomings in our lives and pretend everything is all right when it isn't. In doing so we hide our true feelings to appear more spiritual. Please don't misunderstand what I am saying. I don't think the Scripture is advocating that we reveal all of our past mistakes and secret sins to every other Christian we meet, nor express our emotions in an unrestrained way. That will do nothing but drive us apart. But to be candid, most of us live behind masks. We don't want people to know what's going on inside us because, as John Powell so skillfully pointed out, we are afraid they won't like what they see and will maybe reject us.[5] We hide our true self and say just what we think will create the

**Another way we shade the truth is to tell only what suits our purpose.**

kind of image we want to project. We avoid sharing our feelings of hurt, anger, jealousy, inferiority, frustration or depression, convincing ourselves that it would be better for our image if we keep them to ourselves. But they affect the way we treat each other and they hinder our ability to get along with each other.

**Rarely will we be totally honest about what is going on in our lives. The risk is too great.**

We hold our conversations to the cliché level: "Hi, how are you?" Or to the fact level: news, weather, sports, and unfortunately, people. Occasionally we will rise to the idea and opinion level, so long as we don't think our opinions will alienate the people we want to impress. But seldom will we share our feelings, and rarely will we develop a relationship with anybody where we can be totally honest about what is going on in our lives. The risk is too great.

So my wife and I may be drifting apart. But I'm not going to tell you about it. It will distort the image I want you to have of me. I may be losing my temper with my children, but I'm not going to say anything about it. You may think less of me. I may be struggling with alcohol, drugs, or impure sexual desires, but I can't possibly let anyone know. It could cause me to be rejected by the very people I want to respect me. I may be feeling depressed and down on myself. But I don't want to admit it because it doesn't sound spiritual.

**We can stop living a lie.**

We surely do not need to tell everyone all about our feelings, problems, or faults. That would be presumptuous and boring. But we can stop living a lie. We can share with those who genuinely care that we are having problems and need their prayers. We can be honest with at least one close friend who will encourage us, advise us, pray for us, and hold us accountable for the changes we need to make.

That accountability may be one of our main reasons for hiding the truth. To share the problem obligates us to change, the very thing we have resisted so long. But God says one reason we should speak the truth is because we are members of one another. That seems to be a strange reason. He doesn't remind us of the nature of our God, though the fact that He is a God of truth is a good reason for being truthful. He doesn't point out the damage our lying does to the testimony of Christ to the lost, though that is a good reason. He uses the great truth of our union with each other in the Body.

Because we are all members of one Body, we are members of one another. My finger is a member of my hand, and my hand is a member of my arm, and my arm is a member of my torso, to which both my head and my legs are also connected. Ultimately, every member of the body is a member of every other member. God put them all together in such a way as to function harmoniously and successfully.

If the members of my body start lying to each other, they won't get along very well, and the whole body will suffer. If my eyes see a rut in the road, but they tell my feet that the road is

**We will be of little value to each other if we are not honest.**

smooth, one of my feet may get broken. Or if the hand tells the rest of the body that it is fine when in reality its nerve endings are dead, it will eventually destroy itself to the detriment of the whole body. The members of the body need each other, but they are of little value to one another if they are not honest.

Paul is saying that we are all members of one another. God has put us together to function harmoniously and effectively, and for that reason we need each other. But we will be of little value to each other if we are not honest.

Let's go back to my friend Henry who has such a difficult time telling the truth. He and his wife are believers. They are one in Christ. They belong to each other. They are part of each other, one flesh. They need each other. But they are of little value to each other. In order to minister to one another there must be trust, and Henry's wife has no trust in him at all. He has lied to her so often that she doesn't know whether to believe him or not. He promises he will stop lying, but then she catches him in another untruth, so even his promise turns out to be a lie.

If he tries to reassure her of his love, or encourage her about the future, she finds no consolation at all in his words. How can she ever be sure he is telling her the truth? His attempts to minister to her will be rebuffed. Her hopes will be raised, then dashed to splinters. Her resentment will build. Arguments will become frequent. Their relationship will never improve until Henry puts away lying and establishes a habit of telling the truth.

He has a problem with his friends at church too. They don't trust him either and they doubt much of what he says. Can you imagine him trying to teach a Sunday school class? Or counsel a believer with a problem? They would never know what to believe. He can have no ministry in their lives.

He has a problem with other people as well. Since he thinks nothing of distorting the truth, he suspects that others do the same thing. So he doesn't believe much of what they say to him. He even has a problem accepting what his pastor says when he expounds the Word of God. If there are many others like him in his church, you can be sure it is a sick assembly and will soon be a contentious one, for suspicion and distrust are the seeds of conflict. Let us heed the exhortation of God's Word: "Therefore, laying aside falsehood, speak truth, each one of you, with his neighbor, for we are members of one another" (Eph. 4:25).

What about the other side of dishonesty—living a lie, hiding behind a facade, pretending everything is right in our lives when it isn't, hiding our feelings? How does that affect the Body? For one thing, it discourages others who watch us. They know their lives are not perfect, and if they think ours are, they usually conclude that we are somehow different, in a separate category of super-saints to which they can never attain. They tell themselves they can never be like us so there is no reason to try. It alienates them from us and keeps them from coming to us for help. Far from rejecting us for our truthfulness, people usually respect us more and derive great encouragement from knowing that we struggle with the same weaknesses as they. And they will be able to take advice from us more readily when they know that we have been there. They know that we are aware of what it is like. Truthfulness will help us minister to each other more effectively.

In recent years my wife and I have had the privilege of ministering to missionaries on more than a dozen different fields. In each conference we have taken a session to share the platform and briefly recount the story of our lives, warts and all. We have told of the struggles we have encountered in learning to get along with each other, the arguments and conflicts we have endured, and our failure to meet each

**Truthfulness will help us minister to each other more effectively.**

other's needs. In every case, our honesty has helped the missionaries relate more effectively with us and has opened opportunities for counsel. A number of them have said, "We have had the same kinds of problems, but we never told anyone. What would our supporters back home think if they ever found out? Thanks for being honest."

Not only does our deceitfulness make it impossible for us to minister to others, but it makes it impossible for them to minister to us. Let me illustrate. We seldom go to a doctor unless we have admitted that we are sick. He cannot help us unless we are willing to acknowledge that something is wrong and tell him what hurts. The same thing is true in the spiritual realm. God put the Body together in such a way so that each member can minister to other members. But if we refuse to admit our needs, we cut ourselves off from the help which the rest of the Body can provide. They cannot minister to needs of which they are not aware.

If I have a marital problem, you cannot help me work it out unless you know about it. To cover it up would be like a broken thumb saying, "I don't want the rest of the body to know I'm broken. I'll straighten myself out without their help." That is absurd. A broken thumb cannot straighten itself out without help from the rest of the body. And neither can we work out most of our problems without help from the rest of Christ's Body. Problems will just hang on, making us more edgy and irritable and less able to get along with each other. Truthfulness will help us minister to each other more effectively, and improve the spiritual health of the entire Body.

Another detrimental effect of dishonesty about our feelings and faults is that it keeps us from understanding ourselves. Psychologists tell us that we only understand as much of ourselves as we share with others, and I have found it to be true in my own life. The more of my inner life I share with my wife, the more I begin to understand myself. If we are not transparent with others—have never verbalized our hopes and fears, values and priorities, dreams and aspirations, failures and discouragements, joys and sorrows, needs and wants, feelings and frustrations—we probably do not fully understand ourselves, and therefore we are not growing.

Just admitting what is going on inside of us can help us grow. If I must keep saying, "I feel angry with you," eventually I may have to admit that I am expecting too much from you and have never committed my expectations to God. If I must keep saying, "I feel hurt when you say that," I may have to admit that I am overly sensitive about inconsequential things. When I admit that, I will begin to change. And as I grow, I will be of greater help to others in the Body, and the whole Body will function more harmoniously.

Maybe you are beginning to grasp the importance of truthfulness. It can help bring happiness and harmony to our relationships. We need to begin to put off the old way of life and put on the new, lay aside falsehood and speak the truth, for we are members of one another.

# 7

# AN ENCOURAGING
WORD

W HEN OUR CHILDREN WERE GROWING UP, one of the things Mary and I tried to teach them was unselfish consideration for other people. But I have to admit, I thought very little about how selfish and inconsiderate our *conversations* may have sounded. It did not occur to me that I should be teaching them how to communicate with unselfish consideration for others and then to model it before them—probably because I had never learned much about it myself.

## Considerate Communication

Judging from what I hear, I suspect that there are others who have not learned a great deal about considerate communication either. Some of us have a tendency to interrupt while others are talking, dominate conversations with stories about ourselves, show little interest in what others are saying, get impatient and irritated when they disagree with us, say sarcastic things that offend or belittle, or commit any number of other conversational blunders that demonstrate a gross lack of consideration.

We may have little appreciation for the power of our words. "Who am *I?*" we ask. "Just a little old nobody. It doesn't matter what I say. My words don't affect anybody." But they do! They affect everyone we speak to—absolutely everyone. They have the power to help and heal or to hurt and destroy. "There is one who speaks rashly like the thrusts of a sword, but the tongue of the wise brings healing," wrote King Solomon (Prov. 12:18). Some professing Christians swing verbal swords, piercing the souls of other people, inflicting emotional wounds on their spouses, their children, their neighbors, store clerks, telephone operators, or anyone else who gets in their way.

> **Some professing Christians swing verbal swords, piercing the souls of other people.**

As we have seen, the apostle Paul penned an extended passage on the use of words (Eph. 4:25–32). And in one verse he summed up a number of good communication principles: "Let no unwholesome word proceed from your mouth, but only such a word as is good for edification according to the need of the moment, that it will give grace to those who hear" (Eph. 4:29). Paul established two categories of communication in that verse: unwholesome words and edifying words. The first, he says, should be eliminated entirely from our verbal repertoire. There is no room for even a trace of it. We are to weed it all out, then replace it with the second. Obeying this command could vastly improve our ability to get along with each other. But we need to know what kinds of words each category includes. Let's explore them—first the unwholesome or destructive words, then the edifying or constructive words.

## Destructive Words

The word *unwholesome* means decayed, rotten, or diseased. It is used of rotten or degenerate fruit (Matt. 7:17–18) and rotten or degenerate fish (Matt. 13:48). Unwholesome things are putrid, offensive, useless, worthless, or unprofitable—fit for nothing but the trash heap. But worse, when we put a rotten apple in a barrel with good apples, it corrupts the whole lot. It is not only useless, but injurious and harmful. It affects others adversely. Paul seems to be using the word in this sense of damaging others, because he contrasts unwholesome words with edifying words—words that build up, strengthen and heal. Unwholesome words do just the opposite. They tear down, destroy, offend, and hurt. What kind of words did Paul put in this category? The context reveals some. Lying words can injure (v. 25). Bitter words can injure (v. 31). Angry words can injure (v. 31). Malicious, gossiping words can injure (v. 31). All these are discussed in other chapters. What other kinds of words injure people and relationships? Let's think about a few.

> **Unwholesome things are putrid, fit for nothing but the trash heap.**

*Cutting Words.* Solomon spoke of words that pierce like a sword (Prov. 12:18). David had a problem with people whose tongues cut him. He mentions it several times in the Psalms. For example, he says his former friend Ahithophel, who turned against him, spoke words that were like drawn swords (Ps. 55:21). He spoke of people with swords in their lips and tongues (Ps. 57:4, 59:7, 64:3). We've all known folks who have been endowed with sharp tongues. They have the gift of sarcasm. They are masters of the cut, the chop, the putdown. They may do it to be funny, but they fail to think about how much it hurts the victim. Their verbal assaults smack of the foolish talking or jesting which Paul condemned in Ephesians 5:4.

Some husbands and wives take advantage of social gatherings to cut down their spouses. Rather than lovingly confronting in private and talking issues through where they can explore what one another is thinking and feeling, they find it easier to drop little razor blades into the conversation when their spouses cannot fight back. One sharp-tongued husband said, "Dottie doesn't sleep *too* late. She gets up in time to watch the afternoon soaps on TV." But Dottie was not to be outdone: "Max always remembers my birthday—three months later." And a few more wounds have been inflicted that will arouse antagonism, lead to retaliation, and further decay the relationship. Destructive words! "Let no unwholesome word proceed from your mouth" (Eph. 4:29).

> **"Let no unwholesome word proceed from your mouth."**

*Nagging words.* The book of Proverbs says quite a bit about nagging and its effect: "It is better to live in a corner of a roof, than in a house shared with a contentious woman" (21:9). "It is better to live in a desert land, than with a contentious and vexing woman" (21:19). "A constant dripping on a day of steady rain and a contentious woman are alike" (27:15).

There is a difference between nagging and reminding. A reminder is friendly and free from impatience or irritation. But nagging is a repeated, critical request marked by exasperation and anger. It is exactly what Solomon labeled "contentious." A nag has a tendency to scold, lay blame, make insinuations or accusations. "When are you ever going to paint the house? Don't you care what people think?" That is an attempt to create guilt. "Don't you know any better than to slurp your soup? You eat like an animal." That is an attempt to shame.

I don't know why Solomon only picked on the wives. Maybe it was because he had so many of them! But men can be just as guilty. "I wish you'd lose some weight. I'm ashamed to be seen in public with you." Those words are critical, humiliating, and insulting. They hurt and destroy. "I've told you a hundred times that I don't like my coffee this strong." There is that note of humiliation again. The idea is, "What's the matter with you? Don't you understand English? Can't you remember one simple request? Can't you do anything right?"

Nagging words like that are destructive. They irritate, just like the continual drip, drip, drip of a leaky faucet. They hurt by making other people feel badly. Such words heap guilt on people, cause them to think less of themselves, chipping away at their self worth. Those people probably will strike back in some way in an attempt to restore that injured self worth. The result is usually further rotting of the relationship. It isn't necessary to make people feel badly. When we ask someone to do something, and if they agree to do it but fail, we can remind them lovingly and kindly without communicating disgust, frustration, or humiliation. "Let no unwholesome word proceed from your mouth."

> **There is a difference between nagging and reminding.**

*Exaggerated words.* There is a ramification of the falsehood we discussed in the last chapter which should be mentioned here in connection with words that destroy relationships, and that is exaggerated generalizations that take the form of absolute statements. I'm referring to words like *always* and *never.* "You never take me out to eat." "You always greet me with a gripe of some kind when I come home from work." "All you ever think about is _____" (fill in the blank: food, sex, new clothes, etc.). Absolute statements are seldom true and they tend to arouse antagonism in us. They hurt us, so instead of trying to discover what the real problem is that prompted the statement, we focus on proving the statement wrong, and so repairing our injured self esteem.

When a wife says, "You never take me out to eat," her husband may reply, "Why of course I do. I remember taking you out just six weeks ago. You don't remember anything. And besides that, you don't appreciate anything I do for you." And the fight is on. The foolish thing is that they are fighting about a false issue. The issue is not when they went out to eat last. It is probably that she is feeling neglected or overworked. He needs to be more sensitive to her needs. But if she would try to identify her feelings and her desires, then express them directly, lovingly, and honestly instead of making absolute statements that accuse, there is a good possibility that the relationship would be strengthened rather than strained. "Let no unwholesome word proceed from your mouth."

**Absolute statements are seldom true.**

*Vengeful words.* Peter identified some unwholesome words that injure relationships. "To sum up, all of you be harmonious, sympathetic, brotherly, kindhearted, and humble in spirit; not returning evil for evil, or insult for insult, but giving a blessing instead; for you were called for the very purpose that you might inherit a blessing" (1 Peter 3:8–9). We normally respond to angry accusations *with* angry accusations. We answer putdowns with putdowns, and sarcasm with sarcasm. That is our human nature. "You never listen to me," she charges. "That's because you never say anything that's worth listening to," he responds.

We usually live by the adage, "When hurt, strike back and hurt in return." And it does nothing but intensify our conflicts, until they reach the stage of one couple who stood before a judge seeking a divorce.

"Will you please tell the court what passed between you and your wife during the argument that led to this court action?" "I will," said the husband. "It was a rolling pin, six plates, and a frying pan."

Peter admonishes his readers not return evil for evil or insult for insult. We have a new nature, a supernatural nature which is capable of responding just as the Lord Jesus Himself responded. "And while being reviled, He did not revile in return; while suffering, He uttered no threats, but kept entrusting Himself to Him who judges righteously" (1 Peter 2:23). By consciously depending on His power, not only can we hold back the vengeful words, but we can speak words that will calm the angry accuser, heal the hurts that have been experienced, and strengthen the relationship.

## Constructive Words

We have seen some words that destroy relationships; now let us look at some that heal and strengthen them—constructive words. "Let no unwholesome word proceed from your mouth, but only

> **We normally respond to angry accusations with angry accusations.**

such a word as is good for edification according to the need of the moment, that it may give grace to those who hear" (Eph. 4:29). Here in this one verse are some powerful biblical principles that can solve many of our communication problems. If we use them to govern our words, we shall find our relationships improving overnight. Ask yourself, "Do my words edify—do they build the people in my life rather than put them down?" "Are these words what they need at this particular time?" "Will these words minister grace to them—will they benefit them in some way?"

If a wife says to her husband, "You never listen to me," she surely doesn't need to hear, "You never say anything worth listening to." The first statement is false, but two falsehoods do not produce truth. The second falsehood will do more to hurt and destroy than the first did. What does she need at that moment? Words that build! Here are a few.

*Gentle words.* We mentioned gentle words when we discussed how to deal with the faults of others (chapter 3). But their importance demands some further emphasis. Solomon wrote, "A gentle answer turns away wrath, but a harsh word stirs up anger" (Prov. 15:1). The word *gentle* implies words that are tender, delicate, and mild. Paul said much the same thing: "Be kind to one another, tenderhearted, forgiving each other, just as God in

Christ also has forgiven you" (Eph. 4:32). The same tongue that stirs up strife also can communicate kindness, tenderheartedness, and forgiveness when it is controlled by the Holy Spirit. Gentle words can soothe and quiet the atmosphere after foolish words have been uttered. When passions rage, accusations are made, or unkind taunts hurled, try gentle words. Purposely speak in calm, quiet, kind

> **When passions rage, accusations are made, or unkind taunts hurled, try gentle words.**

tones, and choose words that are non-threatening and non-retaliatory. It will be like pouring cold water on burning coals. It takes two to fight; if one decides there is a better way and refuses to retaliate, there will be no fight.

*Understanding words.* If we are only to speak words that build others up according to their needs, then we obviously must understand those needs. That may require some prayerful thought before we open our mouths. Many of us would rather spew out the first thing that comes to our minds when we are issued an invitation to fight. Solomon has some choice observations about that: "Do you see a man who is hasty in his words? There is more hope for a fool than for him" (Prov. 29:20). "The heart of the righteous ponders how to answer, But the mouth of the wicked pours out evil things" (Prov. 15:28).

Part of that prayerful thought will be an effort to determine exactly what the other person is feeling and trying to communicate to us. They may be saying it rather poorly, but there is probably some need behind it. "You never listen to me" translates into something like, "I don't think you are listening to me attentively enough to make me feel loved and understood—and I'm hurting because of it."

It is unfortunate that we cannot phrase things more carefully and simply say what we feel and what we want instead of accusing, criticizing, manipulating, exaggerating, belittling, nagging, or judging motives. But we all have the problem to some degree, and that should help us try to be more patient with others when they are not communicating properly. It should also help us grasp what is behind their words. Then we can respond with understanding words rather than vengeful words. An understanding response might be, "You may be right. I probably don't listen to you as carefully as I should. And I can understand why that bothers you. It would bother me, too. I really want to do better. Can you suggest some ideas that would help me improve in this area?"

Do you see what you have done? You have assured her that you understand why she is disturbed. You have given her an opportunity to say more about it, which she probably wanted to do and needed to do. You have let her know you are interested in making the changes in your life that will bring her greater happiness. And you have focused on a solution, getting the discussion out of the fruitless realm of blame. That kind of answer will help build her up, meet her needs, and benefit her. It is kind, tenderhearted, and forgiving. And what has it cost you besides giving up a "clever" remark that wasn't true in the first place? Understanding words build up and encourage.

*Appreciative words.* The apostle Paul himself gave us an example of words that edify and benefit. In many of his letters he included words of commendation and appreciation. For example, to the Philippians he wrote, "I thank my God in all my remembrance of you, always offering prayer with joy in my every prayer for you all, in view of your participation in the gospel from the first day until now" (Phil. 1:3–5). To the Thessalonians he wrote, "We give thanks to God

> **There isn't one of us who is so confident and self-assured that he does not need a word of praise periodically.**

always for all of you, making mention of you in our prayers; constantly bearing in mind your work of faith and labor of love and steadfastness of hope in our Lord Jesus Christ in the presence of our God and Father" (1 Thess. 1:2–3). Neither the Philippians nor the Thessalonians were perfect, but Paul praised them before he dealt with their problems. There isn't one of us who is so confident and self-assured that he does not need a word of praise periodically. Without it, we become overwhelmed with self-doubts and are incapable of functioning at peak efficiency.

Some of us seem to think that people will get proud if we compliment them too frequently. Quite the contrary! People often become boastful when they are starved for appreciation. A sincere compliment will encourage them to do even better.

> **People often become boastful when they are starved for appreciation.**

Alan McGinnis relates a study of a second grade class in Wisconsin. The children were getting harder to control, standing up and roaming around the room instead of doing their work. Two psychologists spent several days in the back of the room observing. They observed that 7 times in every 27-minute period the teacher said, "Sit down!" But the roaming continued. They suggested that she increase her commands, and she did, to 27.5 times in 20 minutes. The walking around increased 50 percent. Then they suggested instead that she eliminate the commands entirely and quietly compliment the children who were staying in their seats doing their work. The roaming around decreased 33 percent from what it was originally.[6]

Psychologists tell us that, generally speaking, we need at least four positive statements to balance one word of criticism. Delinquent children report getting approximately one to one. Most of us are the same way. We enjoy cooperating with those who show us appreciation and we resist those who criticize us. It would make a significant improvement in the way we get along with the people we live with and work with if we looked for the positive things in their lives and expressed our appreciation. A husband can say, "That was a great meal. Thanks for the time and effort you put into it." A Sunday school superintendent may say to a teacher, "Thanks for your faithfulness to the class. I always know that you're

**Generally speaking, we need at least four positive statements to balance one word of criticism.**

going to be here unless you've notified me ahead of time." Statements like that communicate an important message. They say, "I care about you. You're important to me. I value you highly." They are constructive words that encourage and build.

This is not the false flattery which some people use to get their own way or obtain some favor in return. The Scripture warns about that: "A flattering mouth works ruin" (Prov. 26:28). But it encourages people when we sincerely commend the praiseworthy things we see in them. Train yourself to look for them in the people around you—the checkout clerk at the grocery store, the difficult neighbor, the usher at church, your spouse, your children, your parents, your employees, your boss. In other words, everyone!

Let's take the Word of God seriously and begin to weigh our words. Weed out those that damage people and cause relationships to decay. Replace them with words that build up, meet needs, and minister gracious benefit to people's lives. We will be the beneficiaries in the end as we experience the joy of harmonious relationships.

# 8

# "YOU MAKE ME SO MAD!"

IT'S SATURDAY AFTERNOON. You've spent all day cleaning house for company on Sunday—vacuuming carpets, scrubbing floors, scouring sinks, polishing appliances. Now it's ready for the white glove inspection—but that's not quite what happens. Instead, your teenage daughter buzzes in from the beach with a cheerful "Hi, Mom," and proceeds to walk the length of the house leaving a trail of sand behind her.

Before you have a chance to open your mouth, your husband comes in from the garage where he has been fixing the transmission in his car, and with his greasy hands he manages to redecorate the kitchen sink, the refrigerator and two cabinet doors, in that order. As though perfectly planned and orchestrated by someone who hates you, ten-year-old Johnny, at that precise moment, loses his grip on a muddy bullfrog he has just brought in from the yard. It plants its marks squarely on your newly-upholstered white living room sofa.

The explosion is violent—your worst in months. You scream, call them names, accuse them of being inconsiderate and uncaring, complain about your status as a slave, and threaten to walk out on them. They make you so mad!

The eruption is over now. The air is quiet and still, but tense. Everybody seems to be avoiding you. You feel lonely and rejected, and very guilty. You did it again; you let your anger get out of control, and it's alienated the people you love.

Anger! Some have called it the greatest curse on interpersonal relationships. Dad may be the angry, hostile one in the family. He rants and raves if somebody interrupts his television viewing or newspaper reading, or leaves his tools out to rust. Or maybe it's one of the kids who blows his fuse if he doesn't get his way.

> **God gets angry about some things, and Christians should, too.**

Home is not the only site for exhibitions of anger. We see it on the job, in the neighborhood, on the playing field, even in church board meetings and congregational business meetings.

What is God's perspective on anger? Let's look at His Word, find out what anger is, what it does, and how we ought to deal with it.

## What Anger Is

The dictionary defines anger as "a strong feeling of displeasure and usually of antagonism." The most common Old Testament word for anger is the same word used for the nostrils. Anger is often revealed by the appearance of nostrils, or by heavy breathing. There are two primary New Testament words, one referring to a passionate outburst, and the other to a settled and lingering frame of mind. God isn't very happy about either one. He tells us to get rid of both. "Let all . . . wrath and anger . . . be put away from you . . ." (Eph. 4:31; see also Colossians 3:8).

But the strange thing is that God tells us in the very same context to *be* angry. "Be angry, and yet do not sin; do not let the sun go down on your anger" (Eph. 4:26). It is actually imperative in the Greek text—not "In your anger do not sin," or "When angry do not sin" as some translations render it, but literally, "Be angry." God gets angry about some things, and Christians should, too.

Jesus gave us an example. There was a needy man in the synagogue. He had a paralyzed hand which Jesus could heal. The Pharisees were watching Jesus, hoping He would heal the man so they could charge Him with breaking the Sabbath. "And after looking around at them with anger, grieved at their hardness of heart, He said to the man, 'Stretch out your hand.' And he stretched it out, and his hand was restored" (Mark 3:5). Jesus was angry with the hypocrisy that considers slavish bondage to manmade religious rules to be more important than showing mercy to a person in need. So He did the loving, caring thing and healed the man, even though it was contrary to their rules. That kind of cold and callous insensitivity which masquerades as spirituality ought to make us angry too, as should evil and injustice of every description. That is God's kind of anger, righteous anger.

## Righteous vs. Sinful Anger

What is the difference, then, between righteous anger and sinful anger? We might suggest several distinctions. For one thing, righteous anger is always unselfish, while sinful anger is selfish. It occurs when our desires, needs or ambitions are frustrated, when our demands are not met, when our expectations are not realized, when our wellbeing is threatened, when our self esteem is attacked, or when we are embarrassed, belittled, or

> **Righteous anger is always unselfish, while sinful anger is selfish.**

inconvenienced. "Why doesn't she do what I tell her to do?" "Why doesn't he clean up his mess when he's finished?" Those things inconvenience us.

A second difference is that righteous anger is always controlled, while sinful anger is often uncontrolled. It causes us to say and do things we are sorry for later, things we never would have said or done had we been in control.

A third contrast is that righteous anger is directed toward sinful acts or unjust situations, while sinful anger is often directed against people. God wants us to hate the sin but love the sinner, just as He does. And that means treating the sinner in kind and caring ways. Sinful anger lashes out against people.

A final distinction is that righteous anger has no malice or resentment and seeks no revenge. In fact, it takes positive action to right wrongs and heal divisions and disagreements. Sinful anger, on the other hand, harbors bitterness and seeks retaliation. "He's not going to get away with that." So we make him pay. The angry tirade itself is designed to punish him, as are the cutting and sarcastic remarks, or the silent treatment that follows, or the malicious gossip we spread, or the way we try to alienate his friends from him. Sinful anger wants to hurt, even destroy.

> **God wants us to hate the sin but love the sinner, just as He does.**

God wants us to be angry, but over the right issues, at the right times, and in the right way. He wants us to get rid of all sinful anger. If we are honest, we would probably admit that less than 2 percent of what we display is righteous anger, while the other 98 percent is sinful anger. It is that sinful anger we want to deal with in the remainder of this chapter—those sinful, selfish, spiteful feelings we express toward people who displease us.

## What Anger Does

If somebody grabs you and begins yelling at you angrily because you accidentally stepped on his toe, a number of physiological changes will begin to take place in your body immediately. Adrenalin will pump into the bloodstream. Blood pressure and heartbeat will increase. The pupils will dilate and the muscles will tense. It is the body's way of readying itself for sudden crisis. That response is involuntary. It will happen whether you want it to or not. It may be a mixture of surprise, fear, anxiety, and anger, but that anger is not sinful. God built the capability to respond that way into your being. The question is, what will you do with that initial wave of emotion? The choice is now yours to make. You have a few moments to evaluate the situation, process the data, and formulate your response. What will it be?

If you decide that the situation warrants venting your anger, that you would be justified in expressing it, you will probably yell right back, insist it was an accident, or that it was really his own fault. Some psychologists say it is good for us to vent our anger, get it out and release the pressure. The problem is that venting it tells the body to maintain emergency status, so it keeps more anger flowing. Furthermore, it establishes more deeply in our brain cells the habit of reacting angrily, making it more difficult to put away all sinful wrath and anger, as the Bible tells us to do.

Furthermore, if we allow that emergency state to continue, it reduces our ability to reason clearly, ultimately upsetting the chemical balance in our bodies and making us physically sick. Doctors suggest that things like migraine headaches, thyroid malfunction, ulcerative colitis, toxic goiters, high blood pressure, ulcers, heart attacks, backaches, rheumatism, arthritis, allergies, indigestion, asthma and many other illnesses can be emotionally induced.

But equally serious is the fact that we will alienate people from us, often the people we love the most. They are the ones on whom we make the greatest demands, from whom we have the highest expectations. Consequently they become the objects of our fiercest anger. It is unrealistic to hurl angry accusations at our loved ones, then expect them to shower love on us in return. They are human too. And a basic human principle revealed in Scripture is that anger begets anger. "A gentle answer turns away wrath, but a harsh word stirs up anger" (Prov. 15:1). "A hot-tempered man stirs up strife, but the slow to anger calms a dispute" (Prov. 15:18). "An angry man stirs up strife, and a hot-tempered man abounds in transgression" (Prov. 29:22).

There is a great deal of contention and strife in Christian churches and homes today because God's people have not dealt with their anger. We hear people say, "But getting angry is the only way I can get any action." So they go on yelling at each other and excusing it. But God's Word says ". . . the anger of man does not achieve the righteousness of God" (James 1:20). We are not really teaching anything by our anger except a poor example that will adversely affect generations to come.

## How to Deal with Anger

> **There are some harmful ways to deal with anger.**

There are some harmful ways to deal with anger. We have already mentioned its unrestrained expression and the damage that does, but there are others. One of the most common ways for Christians to handle it is to deny it. We tell ourselves that Christians aren't supposed to be angry. I'm a Christian, so naturally, I'm not angry. I'm concerned, hurt, disappointed, a bit upset, but not angry.

My "image" as a spiritual Christian requires that I not be angry, so I deny it, or I repress it and drive it deep down inside where it eats at my organs, makes me physically sick, or causes me to get depressed. I store it up until the pressure gets so great that it explodes in a flare-up much out of proportion to the seriousness of the incident. Or I hold it in until I can direct it at some less threatening object. My boss can fire me, so I don't yell back at him—I go home and yell at my wife instead. And.she yells at the kids. And they kick the cat. And the cat scratches the baby, whose developing lungs can make life miserable for everyone.

If we don't let our anger explode, we may let it ooze out in subconscious ways, like being consistently late, or burning the supper, or avoiding people, or pouting, teasing, being sarcastic, forgetting to call, or other such habits that let people know we are angry with them. Those things don't accomplish anything constructive. There are better ways to manage our anger. Paul said to put it away. But how? That is the question that needs to be answered. Let me offer several suggestions.

The first thing we can do is to admit our anger honestly and accept full responsibility for it. That may be difficult to do if we have repressed it or denied it all our lives. But this step is essential. Learn to ask yourself, "What am I feeling right now? Am I angry with that person for what he has done?" Then admit it. Not, "You make me angry." That is an attempt to pin the blame on others, and it is not fair to them. Nobody makes us feel anything! *They* are responsible for their actions, but *we* are responsible for our feelings. We choose to be angry. We could choose to forgive, to act kindly, to speak softly, or to express humor. But if we choose to be angry, we should be willing to say so: "I feel angry when you talk to me like that." We make no sarcastic remarks, no putdowns, no accusations, just an honest statement of fact. We feel angry.

> **We are responsible for our feelings.**

It is amazing how much pressure is relieved by that simple, honest admission. Yet many folks have never thought about being that honest. They have never seen any model other than uncontrolled expression or stifling repression, so they do not know how to be honest. Paul says we are to speak the truth (Eph. 4:25). James says we are to confess our faults to one another (James 5:16). Try it. And when you do, it might also be good to express your desire to overcome the anger. Say something like, "I don't want to feel angry with you. I don't like myself when I'm angry like this. I want to feel close to you and loving toward you." That will also help to expedite the healing process.

A second suggestion for eliminating anger is to examine its cause. God would have us think carefully and deliberately before we speak too quickly. Many passages of Scripture allude to that (compare James 1:19; Prov. 12:16; 14:29; 16:32; 19:11; 29:11). The answer is not to count to ten, but to *think.* The best thing to think about may be the reason for our anger. Almost all anger can be traced to our needs and wants. Christian psychiatrists suggest some common causes:

- *Selfishness:* Our selfish demands are not being met.

- *Perfectionism:* Our perfectionist expectations are not being satisfied, which makes us angry with ourselves and others.

- *Suspiciousness:* We misinterpret the motives or intentions of others. We think they are ignoring us, belittling us, or contradicting us.[7]

We want people to treat us properly and we get angry when they do not, so an important step to resolving our anger is to identify exactly what we want from them.

> **Almost all anger can be traced to our needs and wants.**

Is it attention I want, respect, recognition, appreciation, consideration, love? Do I want to be listened to, to have my opinions regarded as worthwhile, my requests regarded as important? Do I want to be relieved of some of my responsibilities? Do I want my belongings handled with care? Do I want people to be more concerned about my feelings or my convenience? We have all become angry because we expected someone to fulfill some want, and they failed. So identify the desire.

That leads to the third step in resolving the anger. Forgive others for their failure to meet our expectations. We really have no recourse but to forgive them when we realize how much God has forgiven us. And forgiveness can wash the anger right out of our lives. Anger is often an attempt to pay others back for wrongs they commit against us. But if we forgive, we pay for the wrongs ourselves. And since they are paid for, there is no reason to be angry anymore.

Some of us Christians struggle with anger because we have a weak understanding of God's grace. We think that somehow we must perform in order to be accepted by God. So we expect others to perform up to our perfectionist demands before we extend to them our acceptance.

> **Forgiveness can wash the anger right out of our lives.**

If they fail, we think we have the right to punish them with anger. God has accepted and forgiven us, not on the basis of our performance, but on the basis of His grace and His Son's redemptive death at Calvary.

When we understand the immensity of our sin, and the vastness of His forgiving grace, we will stop trying to exact payment from others for all the petty little ways they fail to meet our expectations. We will be able to forgive and our anger will dissolve. We shall deal more fully with forgiveness and its place in our relationships with others in a later chapter. But with that brief word, we should be ready for some preventative medicine.

Step number four in resolving our anger is to express our wishes openly. If we want something from those close to us, or feel that we need something from them, we should say so. Don't play that old game of hide and seek: "If you loved me, you would know what I want." Say it plainly, whatever it is.

"Honey, I would like to go out to eat tonight."

"It's important to me that you throw your dirty clothes in the hamper."

"I'd like you to try to greet me cheerfully when I come home from work. It makes my whole day."

"I want you to say 'I love you,' or 'I'm sorry, I was wrong,' or 'Thank you.'"

**Talk to God about your anger.**

Sometimes people fail to fulfill our wishes because they really do not know what those wishes are. Some have protested when I have made this suggestion to them: "But I've told him a thousand times" or "It doesn't mean anything if I have to tell him." We may have whined, complained, nagged, and accused a thousand times. But that only arouses antagonism and resistance. We need to explain directly, calmly, kindly, and lovingly what we want. And there is a difference! Try talking it through, sharing what you would like, and why it is important to you.

And incidentally, it would be good if we would go through this whole process before bedtime—admitting our anger, examining its cause, forgiving the failures of the other person, and expressing our wishes. Look at it again: "Be angry, and yet do not sin; do not let the sun go down on your anger" (Eph. 4:26). Don't let resentments build up. Talk about the things over which you have gotten angry, and do it before the day is over if at all possible. When we let it linger, it has a way of getting buried in the pile of daily responsibilities and becoming the worm that spoils the relationship.

Maybe we should remind you again that now that you have made your wishes known, you should give others the freedom to fulfill them or not fulfill them. You want that freedom from them, don't you? So extend the same freedom to them. Refuse to lock them into your expectations and demands, to manipulate them into conforming to your will, or to make them feel guilty if they fail. Commit all your expectations to God and let Him give you back through them the things He wants you to have. The Spirit of

God will use that relaxed attitude of submission to help remove anger from your life.

A final suggestion for putting away sinful anger is to seek help from the Lord and from others. This is probably the most important step of all. Talk to God about your anger. Ask Him to give you a clearer understanding of its cause, a greater desire to overcome it, a willingness to forgive others and to yield your expectations to Him. Then invite others to help you overcome it by letting you know when they feel anger coming from you. I have asked my wife to do that. It stops me short. But I usually have to admit, "Yes, I am feeling anger right now." Then I can ask God to help me resolve it, right there on the spot. It works wonders, when I remember to do it!

Anger is the work of the flesh, the old sin nature (see Galatians 5:19–20). It comes naturally. But God wants us to change, and He can help us. "Walk by the Spirit, and you will not carry out the desire of the flesh" (Gal. 5:16). Live in God's presence, depend on His power. Ask Him to make you aware of your anger and help you resolve it. Ask your spouse, your children, and your friends to tell you when they sense anger in you, then turn to God for the victory-producing power which He makes available so that anger and wrath will be put away from you, just as He commands.

# 9

# AS GOD HAS
# FORGIVEN

L ET'S ASSUME THAT YOU HAVE BEEN HURT, more than you ever
thought you could be. A friend has betrayed you by telling
someone else a secret which you had revealed about yourself in
strictest confidence. Now everyone knows it, and you are
ashamed to show your face. How can you ever forgive that blabbermouth?

Or maybe a coworker has presented your idea as if it were his
own. He has taken full credit for it and received all the glory for
it, including a promotion and a raise. Now he is finding it difficult
to look you in the eye. But you don't even care. In fact, you don't
care if you ever see him again. How can you ever forgive him?

The possibilities for other ways to be hurt are endless. Someone lied to you, or spread a false rumor about you, or ruined a

possession, or refused to believe you or listen to you. Your parents are continually trying to manipulate your life. Your ungrateful children have shamed you by repudiating everything you stand for. Your brother has swindled you out of the family inheritance. A so-called "friend" has alienated your spouse's affections. An ex-mate keeps trying to sabotage your life. A pastor has failed to stand by you when you needed him. How can you ever forgive?

> **There is little that affects our relationships so profoundly and adversely as an unforgiving spirit.**

There is little that affects our relationships so profoundly and adversely as an unforgiving spirit. Holding something against someone has a tendency to dominate our lives. We may not even realize it. We think we have it resolved in our minds. But all the time it is eating away at us, affecting our disposition, our physical health, and unquestionably affecting the way we treat the people who hurt us. It may be in small ways—looking the other way when they pass, refusing to smile, maintaining a coolness in our voices. It may be in more extreme ways like anger or malicious gossip. But it is always there, extinguishing the warmth and intimacy we long to enjoy with the people around us.

The apostle Paul made an interesting point about forgiveness in his central passage on human relationships. "Let all bitterness and wrath and anger and clamor and slander be put away from you, along with all malice. Be kind to one another, tenderhearted, forgiving each other, just as God in Christ also has forgiven you" (Eph. 4:31–32). Did you notice how he contrasts destructive attitudes and practices like bitterness, anger, slander, and malice on one hand, with kindness, tenderness, and forgiveness on the other? Would you like to rid yourself of those destructive chains that shackle your freedom to get along with other people? One key that unlocks that chain is forgiveness.

But it is so difficult to forgive, isn't it? "How can I do it?" you ask. The secret is found right here in this verse: "forgiving each other just as God in Christ also has forgiven you." We forgive as God forgives. How is that? If we could learn some of the elements in God's forgiveness, we would know how we can forgive.

> **If we could learn some of the elements in God's forgiveness, we would know how we can forgive.**

## He Is Understanding of Our Weaknesses

Forgiveness is a dominant theme in Psalm 103 (note especially verses 3 and 10 through 13). Notice that in reference to God's being compassionate and pardoning, "For He Himself knows our frame; He is mindful that we are but dust" (Ps. 103:14). In addition, when our Creator became a man in the person of Jesus Christ, He gained from experience what it is like to be human. Hebrews 4:15 says, "For we do not have a high priest who cannot sympathize with our weaknesses, but One who has been tempted in all things as we are, yet without sin." Jesus understands.

Forgiveness begins with learning to be understanding of others. That should not be too difficult. We know what we are like. At least if we are honest

> **Forgiveness begins with learning to be understanding of others.**

with ourselves, we do. We know how proud, how selfish, how spiteful, how jealous, how inconsiderate, and how inept we can be. Why shouldn't we show a little tolerance for those same faults in others? People who refuse to forgive may have the foolish idea that they themselves are almost perfect.

As McGinnis put it, "If we are to forgive freely, we need a tolerance of others as generous as the tolerance we display toward our own errors. It is remarkable how understanding we can be of our own flops in interpersonal dealings—we didn't intend the error, or it happened in a moment of stress, or we weren't feeling right that day, or we'll know better next time. We tend to see ourselves not for what we are but for what we strive to be, whereas we see others for what they are."[8]

Being understanding of others does not always mean that we will agree with them. My wife Mary and I used to go around and around on this. "You don't understand me," she would say. "Of course I do," I would insist. "But if you understood me you would agree with me," she would counter. I didn't think that was necessarily true and I would tell her so. But I have since figured out what our problem was. I understood her, but I was not being very understanding. And there is a difference.

To be understanding is more than comprehending words. It is trying to look at things from the other person's point of view, whether or not we agree with them. It is trying to feel what they are feeling, and accepting their feelings whether or not we consider their feelings well-founded. They can usually sense that attitude in us—or the lack of it. And cultivating that attitude can help us forgive when the need arises.

**Understanding alone is not forgiveness.**

One spiritually-minded young wife shared with us how she managed to forgive her husband when he was curt and irritable with her. She said, "I know that's not the way he wants to be. He wants to be a man who pleases God, and usually he is. Some difficult circumstances have him out of sorts right now." That is what it means to be understanding, and that attitude helped her be forgiving.

But understanding alone is not forgiveness. It is merely an important preparatory step. We see the heart of forgiveness in the next thing God does.

## He Pays for Our Offenses

Have you ever had someone apologize to you, and you responded with something like, "Oh, don't worry about it. It was nothing. It didn't bother me at all"? You probably thought your attitude conveyed genuine forgiveness. But it didn't. In fact, you had probably already complained to several people about what that person did to you, revealing that it really *did* bother you. And it probably affected the way you acted toward the person. Forgiveness is more than pretending the offense didn't happen, or pretending it didn't hurt. Forgiveness is facing the fact that it did happen and admitting that it did hurt, but deciding to pay for the offense ourselves.

> **Forgiveness is deciding to pay for the offense ourselves.**

That is what God did. In Paul's second epistle to the Corinthians he assures them that God had not counted their trespasses against them (2 Cor. 5:19). How could a holy God not do that? Paul explains how. "He made Him [Christ] who knew no sin to be sin on our behalf, so that we might become the righteousness of God in Him" (5:21). He could forgive us because He was willing to bear the penalty of our sin in the person of His Son. As verse 19 also puts it, "God was in Christ reconciling the world to Himself." When an offense is committed, somebody has to pay. When justice prevails, the offender pays. But when forgiveness is granted, the offended party himself pays.

Our sins offended God's infinite holiness, but He Himself paid the debt they incurred. When Jesus Christ bowed His head in death, He cried, "It is finished." That is one word in the Greek text, a word sometimes used in business transactions of the day. When written across a bill it meant, "Paid in full." There is nothing we can add to what Christ has done, nothing we can do to deserve *His* forgiveness, and nothing we can pay to secure it. Christ has paid for our offenses in full and God has, in His grace, absolved us of our guilt forever (if we have personally availed ourselves of Christ's substitutionary and redemptive payment for our sins). Grace is at the heart of forgiveness.

> **When justice prevails, the offender pays. But when forgiveness is granted, the offended party himself pays.**

Our failure to appreciate this truth is one of the major reasons we find it so difficult to forgive others. That was the point of Jesus' parable of the unmerciful servant (Matt. 18:23–35), which He told in answer to Peter's question about how many times he had to forgive a brother who sinned against him. It was the story of a king who wanted to settle accounts with his slaves. One of them owed him the enormous sum of $10,000,000. There was no way he could possibly repay it, so the king commanded that he and his entire family be sold in order to recoup a little of his loss.

"So the slave fell to the ground and prostrated himself before him, saying, 'Have patience with me, and I will repay you everything'" (v. 26). He wants an extension of time. He thinks that given enough time he can pay his debt. "And the lord of that slave felt compassion and released him and forgave him the debt" (v. 27). He got a whole lot more than an extension of time. In an act of unparalleled mercy and grace, the king cancelled his entire debt, forgiving him fully. He himself paid his slave's debt in full.

That king pictures God, and what he did dramatizes the tremendous price God paid for our eternal forgiveness. But in the story, it appears that the slave never fully grasped what the king had done. He never received the king's forgiveness. He still thought he had to pay, and that somehow he could pay. That is the point of what follows. He went out and found one of his fellow slaves who owed him the equivalent of about $20, and he grabbed him by the throat, and began to choke him and demand his money. His fellow slave pleaded with him to have patience, promising to repay him everything he owed. But he was unwilling. He threw his fellow slave in prison until he should pay back his debt. What a hypocrite to be forgiven so much but refuse to forgive so little!

That is exactly what some of us professing Christians are doing. We have little understanding of the reality and immensity of God's gracious forgiveness. And because we misunderstand God's grace and think we have to pay Him off with a certain level of performance for the forgiveness He has offered us, we think we have the right to turn around and demand payment from others before we have to forgive them. They have wronged us, so they owe us, and now they have to pay. And we are going to see that they do in one way or another. So we begin making our demands. We may demand an apology, insist that they crawl back to us and admit their blame. "It's all your fault," we insist. "Admit it." We may demand that they try to undo the wrong they have committed against us to change the unchangeable past. We may demand a guarantee that they will never do it again.

If they will not pay what we think they owe, we may punish them. We can do that with an angry tirade, or we can change our tactics and snub them with the silent treatment, acting as though they weren't there. In addition to that, we will probably tell others about the awful things they have done to us so we can put them in a bad light with their friends. That will fix them. We may even take them to court. But one way or another, we are going to make them pay.

That was the problem in Corinth. Believers were taking each other to court. They had not grasped the meaning of God's grace and the reality of how much God had forgiven them. "Why not rather be wronged?" Paul asked. "Why not rather be defrauded?" (1 Cor. 6:7). It is far better to suffer insult, injury, loss, or damage ourselves than risk the slightest possibility of inflicting it on other believers. That is the essence of forgiveness—paying the damages ourselves, canceling every demand, giving up the right to seek any kind of revenge, blatant or subtle, overt or covert. It is giving up our right to hurt others simply because they have hurt us. That is what God does for us, and that is what He wants us to do for others.

Do you remember what happened to the slave who refused to forgive in Jesus' parable? When his fellow slaves saw what he had done, they were grieved and reported it to the king. He called the slave to him and said, "You wicked slave, I forgave you all that debt because you pleaded with me. Should you not also have had mercy on your fellow slave, in the same way that I had mercy on you?" (Matt. 18:32–33). And he handed him over to the torturers until he should repay all that he owed. Jesus concludes the story by saying, "So shall My heavenly Father also do to you, if each of you does not forgive his brother from your heart" (Matt. 18:35). That is a frightening thought. We are not sure who the torturers are, but some have suggested that they are the inner tormentors that plague the person who refuses to forgive—the acid of anger, resentment, bitterness, malice, guilt, depression, and despair that eats at us and destroys us. What a horrible plight!

Dr. S. I. McMillen tells of a college student who came to his office suffering from burning sensations in his upper abdomen, as well as acute indigestion. Medication did not seem to help, and the doctor was baffled with the case. One day a fellow student reported to him of hearing the young man give a heated diatribe denouncing some people who had defrauded his grandfather, and with whom he was determined to get even one way or another. The doctor confronted the student with his grudge and encouraged him to forgive, but he refused. His condition eventually got so bad that he had to drop out of school.[9] As much as forgiveness may cost us, the expense is usually greater when we withhold it, particularly in terms of inner tormenters.

## He Forgets Our Wrongs

Love "does not take into account a wrong suffered" (1 Cor. 13:5). The word Paul used in that description of love was an accounting term used of entering an item on a ledger so it would not be forgotten. When a person takes account of a wrong committed against him, he marks it down in his mental calculator so he can use it when he needs it. God does not do that. He chooses to push the "clear" button on His calculator and forever lose that derogatory information. Several times in Scripture He assures us that He will remember our sins no more (Jer. 31:34; Heb. 10:17; Isa. 43:25). How does God forgive? When He forgives, He forgets, and we need to do the same.

But now we have a problem, because it appears as though our mental calculator has no "clear" button. We cannot actually erase an event from our brain cells. Medical science tells us it is always there, able to be recalled, unless of course we have shock treatments or brain surgery, neither of which is recommended to help us forgive properly. What then does it mean for us to forget?

First of all, when we truly forgive, the wrong will not dominate our thoughts anymore. When it comes to our minds, we will be able to dismiss it promptly. We won't keep reliving it and talking about it to others. Some people say they have forgiven, but they can talk about little else. They want to keep rehearsing the awful thing that was done to them. Their inability to stop thinking about it and talking about it exposes their lack of forgiveness.

> **Some people say they have forgiven, but they can talk about little else.**

Second, the offense won't hurt anymore. The fact will be there, but the deep emotions will be gone. We can think of it without bitterness or resentment, without feeling the pain all over again.

And third, we will be able to treat the offender as though the offense never happened. Not pretend that it never happened—it did happen, and we need to be honest about that. But treat him as though it never happened. If we forgive as God forgives and keep no record of the wrong, then it cannot possibly affect our actions. We will be free to reach out with warmth, kindness, openness, and trust to restore the relationship. And that actually leads us to the last element of God's forgiveness that we need to understand.

## He Seeks Our Fellowship

The aim of forgiveness is reconciliation. There is no such thing as forgiveness that says, "Well, I'll forgive him, but I don't ever want to be close to him again. Let him live his life and I'll live mine." That is not the way God's forgiveness operates. He seeks out sinful people like us (see Luke 19:10). He actually reaches out to His enemies and endeavors to reconcile them to Himself (Rom. 5: 10).

> **Reconciliation is a two-way street.**

But as you might expect, reconciliation is a two-way street. In order for the sinner to be reconciled to God, he must acknowledge his sin and repent. And there is a lesson in that for us. One-sided forgiveness on our part may relieve the bitterness in us and drain some of the tension out of the relationship. But there can never be true reconciliation until there has been loving confrontation and repentance, until the wrong has been worked through together, until both parties have acknowledged their wrong and both are willing to trust each other again. We cannot demand that other people repent. We cannot insist that they work through the wrong with us. But we can acknowledge our part of the wrong, then reach out to them and let them know we are willing to work at reconciliation. That is all God asks of us.

> **If you are the offender, your responsibility is to take the initiative.**

If you are the offended party, your responsibility is to take the first step. "And if your brother sins, go and show him his fault in private; if he listens to you, you have won your brother" (Matt. 18:15). You must do it in love and meekness, but you must do it.

If you are the offender, again, your responsibility is to take the initiative. "Therefore, if you are presenting your offering at the altar, and there remember that your brother has something against you, leave your offering there before the altar, and go; first be reconciled to your brother, and then come and present your offering" (Matt. 5:23–24).

If your brother has something against you, then evidently you have offended him, and you are to make the first move. The Scripture knows nothing like, "Well it was more his fault. He should come to me." God wants alienated brothers and sisters in Christ to be reconciled. And whichever role you fit, the offended or the offender, if you want to obey the Word of God you will reach out. Biblically, it is always your move.

Is there a wall between you and some other believers? You have been hurt, more than you ever thought you could be. God wants you to forgive just as He has forgiven you in Christ. Be understanding toward them in their weakness. Be willing to pay for their offenses in full. Put the wrong behind you permanently, and then reach out in love to effect a reconciliation. You will contribute to greater harmony in the body of Christ. You will feel better emotionally and physically. You will enjoy life more. You will find greater reality in your walk with God. You will experience greater effectiveness in your spiritual service. And God will be glorified!

> **Is there a wall between you and some other believers?**

# 10

# SWEET
# AS HONEY

CHILDHOOD MEMORIES, some pleasant and some unpleasant, linger in our minds no matter how old we become. I can still remember the neighbors on our block where I grew up. Right next door to us was one of the nicest older couples I have ever known. Though my friends and I got a little noisy at times, or thoughtlessly ran across their beautifully manicured lawn, they were always kind and friendly. Long after I had married and moved many miles from home, I still considered them as friends. When I returned to my hometown for a visit I would stop in and say hello.

Next door to them lived one of the grumpiest men I have ever known. I can never remember hearing him say a kind word during the entire ten years I lived in that neighborhood. If my ball accidentally rolled on his grass, he would give me an unforgettable tongue-lashing. When I walked by his house with my friends, he would scowl at us as though we were the enemy bent on invading his property and killing a blade of his precious grass. I can't remember his name, but I can remember hoping I would never grow up to be an old grouch like him.

Nearly every child knows somebody like that. They have a tendency to become the target of childhood pranks, and that just makes them more cranky. But their irritability is not only directed at the neighborhood kids; they get out of sorts with their own families, with their in-laws, with people at work, people at church, and anyone else who crosses them. When you talk to them you usually find out how bad things are going for them, how poorly they have been treated, how unhappy they are about the way things have turned out, and what a mess the world is in. Being near them is about as enjoyable as hugging a porcupine. You seldom hear a pleasant word from them. And the sad thing is, some of them claim to know the Lord.

> **Did you know that God puts a premium on pleasant words?**

Did you know that God puts a premium on pleasant words? "Pleasant words are a honeycomb, sweet to the soul and healing to the bones" (Prov. 16:24). We all know that too much honey can make us sick. But Solomon is not talking about the flattering, fawning, sickening sweet gush that turns our stomachs. He is talking about words that are born in love, that breathe love—agreeable, gracious, friendly, kind words that demonstrate unselfish concern for the welfare of others. They are the opposite of negative, critical, complaining, quarrelsome words. They are sweet to the soul. That is, they minister to our innermost being, lifting our spirits and brightening our lives. And they are health to our bones. That is, they contribute ultimately to our physical wellbeing. Just as surely as unpleasant words can make us sick, pleasant words can help to keep us healthy.

Some of us have never considered this far-reaching effect of our words. Think of it! By our words we can contribute to health and happiness, or to sickness and sadness. It might be wise to learn how to use that awesome power properly before somebody gets seriously hurt or emotionally maimed for life. Let's discuss the nature of pleasant words so we can use them to minister health and happiness to our own lives as well as to those around us.

> **Some of us have never considered this far-reaching effect of our words.**

## They Are Agreeable

One of the basic meanings of this word *pleasant* is "agreeable." It was used by David of his friendship with Jonathan. "I am distressed for you, my brother Jonathan; you have been very *pleasant* to me. Your love to me was more wonderful than the love of women" (2 Sam. 1:26, italics added). Those two men enjoyed a beautiful harmony between them. They thought much the same way, had similar likes and dislikes, had a kindred spirit. The result was that they spoke agreeably to one another, and that was pleasant to both of them.

Being agreeable does not mean that we never have differing opinions. It means we have a positive outlook rather than negative. We emphasize areas on which we agree rather than look for things at which we can pick and complain. We avoid making an issue over minor details. We maintain good feelings and accepting attitudes toward people even when we do not concur with everything they say or do. And we speak kindly and amiably to them under all circumstances.

> **Being agreeable does not mean that we never have differing opinions.**

We all know negative people, don't we? Not me, or you, of course. But someone else! It is always someone else, isn't it? And we don't enjoy being with them, do we? If we have a new idea, they will usually oppose it. It is like an automatic response with them. If we have an opinion, it is not exactly right and they will insist on correcting it. If we tell a story, our details will be a little mixed up and they will straighten us out. If we try to do a job, they will tell us there is some better way to do it. If we propose a solution, it won't work, or it will cost too much. Something will be wrong with it—we can count on it. These people spend their lives looking for problems rather than solutions.

Negative parents chip away their children's self respect and self worth. The kids feel as though they can never please. Negative teachers discourage their students from learning. The students feel that they can never do well enough. Negative church members subdue the enthusiasm of others in the assembly and grind the progress of God's work to a halt. Their disagreeable words are like ice water on warm glowing embers, and they destroy the health of a congregation. But "pleasant words are a honeycomb, sweet to the soul and healing to the bones."

> **Joyful words cheer people up and gladden their hearts.**

## They Are Joyful

Pleasant words are also joyful words. "Anxiety in a man's heart weighs it down, But a *good* word makes it glad" (Prov. 12:25, italics added). "Good" is a synonym for "pleasant" which emphasizes joyfulness. And joyful words cheer people up and gladden their hearts. Some Christians have the strange idea that it is more spiritual to be gloomy and glum, and that the closer a person walks with God the more he will look like he has been sucking lemons. We seem to view ourselves as sanctimonious rainclouds whose job is to dampen every smile. But that isn't quite the picture the Bible paints.

"A joyful heart makes a cheerful face" (Prov. 15:13). God takes pleasure in a happy heart and a happy face. "All the days of the afflicted are bad, But a cheerful heart has a continual feast" (Prov. 15:15). In other words, it savors all of life, just as a connoisseur of fine food savors every meal. "A joyful heart is good medicine" (Prov. 17:22). Cheerfulness is therapeutic.

When Norman Cousins, former editor of *The Saturday Review* was told in 1964 that he was suffering from a rare disease of the connective tissue that was causing his spine literally to come apart, his chance of full recovery was estimated at one in one hundred. He asked for some old comedy films and found that ten minutes of genuine belly laughter gave him at least two hours of pain-free sleep. Very gradually, to the astonishment of his doctor, he began to improve. Sixteen years after his prognosis, he was free of pain, riding horses and playing tennis and golf.

**We would relax more and enjoy each other more if we learned to laugh more.**

God said it thousands of years ago, "A joyful heart is good medicine." And there is something that can make our hearts more joyful than old comedy films. David told us about it: "The righteous man will be glad [joyful] in the LORD" (Ps. 64:10). When we know the Lord we have something to make us merry. There is every evidence that the Lord Himself has a sense of humor, and there is no reason why the people who know Him shouldn't cultivate it as well. We would relax more and enjoy each other more if we learned to laugh more, even laugh at our own blunders and our own perfectionist demands.

Some of the most memorable times we have had as a family have been the times when our house was filled with raucous laughter, when we laughed so hard the tears flowed and our stomachs ached. There was nothing sacrilegious about it. It drew us closer. I am not advocating coarse joking that is inappropriate, offensive or insulting. I am talking about the ability to see the comical side of life and express it with lighthearted wit and wholesome humor. Some Christians could use a good dose of laughter.

I know that there are some folks who will not like what I am saying. They will insist that the Christian life is no laughing matter, that we ought to be dead serious about it. And we *should* be serious. But that is no reason to walk around with a frown, looking for somebody who is having fun so we can give him a stern lecture. That isn't spirituality. It is probably just a miserable disposition that resents anybody else being happy. Pleasant words are joyful words, "a honeycomb, sweet to the soul and healing to the bones."

> **Some Christians could use a good dose of laughter.**

## They Are Thankful

The psalmist teaches us something else about pleasant words. "Praise the LORD! For it is good to sing praises to our God; for it is pleasant and praise is becoming" (Ps. 147:1). Praise is pleasant, and it is more than parroting "Praise the Lord" to your friends. Praise is speaking with approval and thanksgiving about God, who He is and what He has done. While it is not identical to thanksgiving, praise involves a thankful spirit. It may be expressed directly to God, such as, "You're a good God, and I am grateful to you for these good things you have done." Or it may be expressed to others, such as, "Let me tell you about God's grace and some of the gracious things He has done for me."

Paul said much the same thing. "Let your speech always be with grace, as though seasoned with salt, so that you will know how you should respond to each person" (Colossians 4:6). Whenever we open our mouths to speak, God wants our words to be saturated with grace. That means gracious, attractive, favorable, kind, and filled with gratitude. Gratitude and thanksgiving are basic elements of the word *grace.* Our conversations should be generously punctuated with thanksgiving and praise.

More thanksgiving and praise would help to transform our gloomy dispositions and improve our relationships with other people. It is impossible to speak of who God is and what He has done, and then go on complaining about circumstances and criticizing people. It is impossible to have true gratitude in our hearts to God, then go on grumbling and griping. Pleasant words are thankful words, "a honeycomb, sweet to the soul and healing to the bones."

## They Are Hopeful

Pleasant words will also be hopeful, not preoccupied with the gloomy side of life but anticipating God's best. If there is one thing the child of

> **Whenever we open our mouths to speak, God wants our words to be saturated with grace.**

God should have, it is hope. We know a God who controls all things and who promises to work everything together for good. As He promised the Jews in exile through Jeremiah, "'For I know the plans that I have for you,' declares the LORD, 'plans for welfare and not for calamity to give you a future and a hope'" (Jer. 29:11). He plans for our wellbeing and promises us a bright future.

Believers can anticipate the very best. But you would never know it to hear some of them talk. Listen to them moan: "Things are bad. And we haven't seen anything yet. They're going to get worse." And they can give you all the facts and statistics to prove that they are going to get worse. They have appointed themselves as official bearers of bad tidings, and they proceed to infect the body of Christ with their pessimism and despair. And that is anything but pleasant.

We have good news to cheer us. God is at work in our midst and in our lives "both to will and to work for His good pleasure" (Phil. 2:13). I know what some will say: "Yes, but . . ." The *Yes, But Brigade* tells you all about the pitfalls, the problems, the obstacles, the unanswered questions and the potential defeats. They are convinced that every cloud has a darker lining than it appears to have, and that behind every cloud is . . . another cloud. If you tell them that God has the power to make their marriage happy and successful, they will probably reply, "Yes, but my spouse is unwilling to make any changes."

If you tell them that God can supply their material needs, they will answer, "Yes, but you don't realize how bad the economic outlook is."

> **We have good news to cheer us. God is at work in our midst and in our lives.**

If you tell them that God can save their loved one, they will offer this happy information: "Yes, but you don't understand how antagonistic he is."

If you remind them that God can help them overcome their depression, they will complain, "Yes, but I've been this way for ten years now." If we keep talking about the worst that could possibly happen, it probably will.

The psalmist had the answer to pessimism. "Why are you in despair, O my soul? And why are you disturbed within me? Hope in God, for I shall again praise Him, the help of my countenance, and my God" (Ps. 43:5). Believe that God can accomplish the very best. Put your hope in Him. Talk about the good things that He can do. Pleasant words are hopeful words, and they are like "a honeycomb, sweet to the soul and healing to the bones."

Could it be that you have been sowing seeds of dissension with a negative, irritable, critical, complaining and gloomy attitude? If you asked your family and friends to rate you on the pleasantness of your words, would they give you a failing grade? But you would like to change. You would like to have pleasant words come out of your mouth. What can make it happen?

The Lord Jesus put His finger on the key factor when He said, "The mouth speaks out of that which fills the heart" (Matt. 12:34). In order to speak pleasant words we will need to feed pleasant thoughts into our minds and meditate on them until they become part of our lives. That may not be easy to do. Some of us have been thinking unpleasant thoughts for years. We may have had a poor example to follow from our parents. We saw them get irritable, heard them fuss, argue, criticize, accuse, grumble, complain, worry, and insist that nothing was going to turn out right. So we naturally assumed that was the thing to do.

> **The psalmist had the answer to pessimism: Hope in God.**

In addition, they may have directed some of their unpleasant words at us. Few of us realize how much our personalities have been shaped by our subconscious struggle to gain the approval of our parents. We may have become obsessive, compulsive perfectionists who thought they would commend us if only we did a little better. That made us demanding and critical of ourselves and others. Our failure to measure up to their standards may have filled us with false guilt and a tendency to lay guilt on others. It may have made us angry and resentful, with an inclination to lash out at the whole world. It is difficult to overcome attitudes that were formed in those early years, but it can be done. God's power is available to change us, to give us pleasant dispositions that will become the source of pleasant words that minister health.

It depends initially on our desire to change. If we are satisfied to remain as we are, we will not change. If it doesn't matter to us that our unpleasant words are hurting our spouses, damaging our children, alienating our friends, or disrupting God's work, we will go right on talking as we always have. Change is usually painful, and we will not subject ourselves to that pain unless there is an overpowering desire to be the people God wants us to be.

> **If we are satisfied to remain as we are, we will not change.**

That is basically a matter of yieldedness. It begins when we yield our bodies to God as a living sacrifice. It continues as we reprogram our minds according to God's Word. And it results in knowing and doing the complete will of God (Rom. 12:1–2). That will include speaking to one another with gracious and pleasant words. If the desire is there, yield your will to the Lord Jesus Christ. Then you will be ready to let Him reprogram your mind and change your disposition through the application of His life-changing principles.

# 11

# CLEANING UP
# THE SOURCE

NOTHING IS MORE REFRESHING after a long summer hike than sitting down in the shade beside a sparkling brook and enjoying a leisurely drink of cool, clear water—but how distressing it would be to then discover that the water is contaminated (in all probability because its source is polluted).

In similar manner, nothing is more refreshing to a Christian who is struggling with the problems of daily living than to sit down with a fellow believer and hear pleasant words that encourage and strengthen the spirit. It is like a cool, refreshing drink of water. But how distressing it would be to hear negative, critical, complaining, or quarrelsome words instead. It would be like drinking contaminated water. Jesus told us what the problem is. The source is contaminated. "For the mouth speaks out of that which fills the heart" (Matt. 12:34).

The apostle James was concerned about professing Christians whose lives have presumably been changed by the Spirit of God, but from whose mouths come bitter words. "But no one can tame the tongue; it is a restless evil and full of deadly poison. With it we bless our Lord and Father, and with it we curse men, who have been made in the likeness of God; from the same mouth come both blessing and cursing. My brethren, these things ought not to be this way. Does a fountain send out from the same opening both fresh and bitter water?" (James 3:8–11).

The word "bless" is used basically two ways in Scripture. When God blesses us it means He is benefitting us in some way. When we bless God we are speaking well of Him. We see both concepts used in Ephesians 1:3: *"Blessed* be the God and Father of our Lord Jesus Christ, who has *blessed* us with every spiritual blessing in the heavenly places in Christ" (emphasis added).

Most of us Christians speak well of God, but we do not always speak well of, or speak well to, other believers. In fact, we may even curse them. To curse means literally "to wish or pray down." It does not require putting a magical hex on somebody, nor does it necessarily involve profanity or blasphemy. It is the desire that harm or ill will come down on someone. James is probably using the term to include words that cause other people harm, whether we wish them to or not. That could involve any destructive words, such as angry, critical, cutting, accusing, belittling, or gossiping words. They cause harm. It doesn't make any more sense for harmful words to come from the same mouth from which words of praise to God come, than for contaminated water to come from a pure source. What is the problem?

> **Most of us Christians speak well of God, but we do not always speak well of other believers.**

All of us struggle with areas of selfishness, self-doubt, insecurity, fear, guilt, anxiety, and complexes of various descriptions.

To protect ourselves, we sometimes lash out with words that wound others. Is it possible to be transformed into a pleasant person whose words consistently bring joy and encouragement to others instead of hurt? James certainly thought so. When he described the enigma of blessing and cursing coming from the same mouth, he said, "My brethren, these things ought not to be this way." Evidently Christians can change. But how?

We saw in the last chapter that change begins when we yield our wills to the Lord Jesus Christ. His Spirit is then free to take control of the heart, the source or fountain of our words, and send out sweet water instead of bitter. He helps us relate to people as He Himself would relate to them—lovingly, kindly, and graciously. In other words, He changes our temperaments.

This does not mean we suddenly attain perfection. As a matter of fact, we will never attain perfection in this life. There are no perfect people on earth. But our goal should be consistent growth. Growth comes gradually, but it will come! As we allow the Spirit of God to apply the principles of His Word to our lives, our temperaments will improve. The fountain will be purified, and as a result we will learn to talk to each other more pleasantly. There are at least three ways we can help clean up the source.

> **Our goal should be consistent growth.**

## Understand Your Position as a Child of God

The experts tell us that one of the basic prerequisites to good communication is the possession of a healthy self-concept. People who don't like themselves, who feel they are not very good or unworthy of being loved and accepted, find it difficult to love and accept others or to relate to them in healthy ways. They may be filled with resentment which surfaces in angry, cutting remarks. They may test other people's love by pushing them to the limit with questions, accusations, or irresponsible behavior just to see if they really care. And they tend to misjudge other people's motives.

For example, a husband may be learning that his wife needs tangible expressions of affection, so he stops on his way home from work to buy her a box of candy, her favorite kind. Because of her poor self image, she finds it difficult to accept his token of affection with gratitude. She doesn't feel worthy of his love, but instead of admitting her feelings of inadequacy she will probably insinuate that his expression of love is not genuine by saying something like, "What are you after this time?" *His* self esteem isn't very high either, so instead of responding with good-natured humor he will probably fly off the handle to demonstrate how hurt he is and to punish her for doubting his intentions. "You never appreciate anything I do. See if I ever buy you candy again." The evening is in shambles and the whole relationship is close to collapse.

Christian psychologist Lawrence Crabb suggests that a sense of personal worth is our most important emotional need, and that two factors contribute to that sense of personal worth. One is *security*—being unconditionally loved and accepted and having a sense of belonging. The second is *significance*—having importance and respect, feeling that we are making some profitable contribution, that we really matter to someone, and that we are capable of handling our situation in life. Women tend to need security more than significance, while men tend to need significance more than security. God assures us in His Word that both of those needs can be met in Him.[10]

> **Women tend to need security more than significance; men tend to need significance more than security.**

Much of our unhappiness—and consequently many of the unpleasant and unproductive words we speak—can be traced to our dependence on people and circumstances instead of on God for the fulfillment of these needs. If our circumstances are trying, we feel at liberty to get irritable. If people fail to treat us as we want them to, we feel justified in wounding them with words. The key to change is to understand our position as children of God.

God created us individually (Ps. 139:13–16). As His children, we are continually in His thoughts (Psalm 139:17–18). He loves us dearly (John 16:27), and nothing can separate us from His love, absolutely nothing (Rom. 8:38–39). We are accepted in His beloved Son (Eph. 1:6), and He will never cast us out (John 6:37). We have been forgiven of all our sins (Col. 2:13), born into His eternal family (John 1:12), made co-heirs with Christ (Rom. 8:16–17), and given a vital and worthwhile role to fill in carrying out His purposes (1 Cor. 12:7, 22). He values us highly, going so far as to call us His own glorious inheritance (Eph. 1:18). He says we are complete in Christ (Col. 2:10), which means that in Him we have everything we need to sustain us emotionally and spiritually in time and for eternity. That means we can depend on Him to meet our basic and fundamental needs for security and significance rather than strive to have them met by others.

Think about how this works in everyday living. Maybe a husband leaves dirty dishes lying around the family room for the wife to clean up. In her lack of security she interprets that to mean, "He doesn't really care about me because he makes unnecessary work." She becomes resentful, and her resentment surfaces not only by nagging him about the dishes but by complaining about other things—the time he spends watching TV, the way he hung the picture, the people he wants to invite for dinner, the little jobs around the house which he has neglected. She feels that her worth as a person depends on the assurance of her husband's love, expressed as she thinks it should be expressed. It would be good if he were more considerate and took his dishes to the kitchen. But her unpleasant reactions would be eliminated if she learns to find her security in the Lord instead of in her husband, and if she understands who she is in Christ and begins to enjoy the worth He places upon her as His very own.

The same thing goes for her husband. He may decide she doesn't respect him because of the innocent comment she made about not having enough money for the new dress she wanted. "She doesn't think I earn enough money. She probably wishes she had married that guy who became a doctor." So he strikes back by criticizing her parents, or complaining about her housekeeping, and life becomes unpleasant for both of them. All of that could be avoided if he learns to find his significance in the Lord and to consciously enjoy the value of being God's child.

Much of our destructive communication occurs when we suspect that our worth is being questioned. God wants us to help each other and minister to each other's needs, but learning to depend on Him alone for our security and our significance would help to improve our temperaments and sweeten our words. It's one way to clean up the fountain.

## Apply the Word of God to Your Life

The Bible is God's operating manual for the human machine He created. He knows how we will function most effectively, and we would be wise to read His instructions. A proper understanding and application of Scripture can make us delightful people whose words are pleasant and edifying. Jeremiah said it best. "Your words were found and I ate them, and Your words became to me a joy and the delight of my heart" (Jer. 15:16). Building the Scriptures into the fabric of our being, learning to think as God thinks and to view things as God views them can fill us with joy. And we will discover, as the people of Nehemiah's day did, that the joy of the Lord is our strength (Neh. 8:10). We shall be strong enough both spiritually and emotionally to avoid the pitfalls that corrupt our communication.

> **The Bible is God's operating manual for the human machine He created.**

Let me suggest an example. Things have not been going too well for you at work. You have made a couple of little mistakes and your supervisor has overreacted and jumped all over you. But this time it is unbearable. He is berating you in front of the other employees, telling you how stupid you are and threatening to fire you. The worst part is that others were just as responsible for the mistake as you were, and he is not saying a thing to them. Emotions are raging inside you— anger that almost approaches hatred, fear that you might lose your job, embarrassment in front of the others, resentment toward other employees who aren't saying a word about their share of the blame, dread of what your wife is going to say if you get fired, anxiety about the future, and so on.

You want to tell your boss exactly what you think of him and remind him of the stupid things he has done. You would like to tell him that he can have his dumb old job. But you are a believer! You remember that your security and significance are found in the Lord, not in this job, not in what this man thinks of you, not even in what your wife says to you. And you have been memorizing the Word of God, meditating on it, thinking through its application to your life and the specific ways it should affect your behavior.

James 3:10 comes to your mind: "From the same mouth come both blessing and cursing. My brethren, these things ought not to be this way." Matthew 5:44 comes to your mind: "Love your enemies, bless them that curse you, do good to them that hate you, and pray for them which despitefully use you, and persecute you" (KJV). And rather than vent your anger, you say something like, "I understand why you feel so strongly about this. I want to do everything in my power to see that it doesn't happen again. Can you give me a few suggestions to help me?"

Some will protest, "But I don't feel like being nice. Isn't it hypocritical to say something nice when you feel nasty?" Doing what God wants us to do is not hypocrisy; it is obedience. It is helpful to understand exactly what we are feeling and to admit it honestly to ourselves, but it is more important at the moment to think properly and act properly. It is difficult to control our feelings, but we *can* control our thoughts and our actions. Thinking properly and acting properly will eventually transform our feelings, and maybe even our temperaments.

God wants us to act toward others as we would act if we were genuinely interested in their wellbeing (even if we are not). Their positive response will bring such satisfaction to us that we may find we *want* to be nice to them. Soon we are beginning to feel kindly toward them and genuinely interested in them. And that helps us feel better about our-selves. Applying the Word of God to our lives can actually improve our temperaments. And that is going to help us speak more pleasantly and kindly.

> **Thinking properly and acting properly will eventually trans-form our feelings.**

## Be Committed to Building Relationships

It seems to me that most troubled couples really want their mar-riages to succeed. They do love each other and long for an intimate and happy relationship, but their basic temperaments and emotional needs cause them to continue saying things to each other that drive them apart. The problem is that each one is more committed to fulfilling his or her own needs than fulfilling the needs of the other and building their relationship. In the middle of a discussion about matters of conscience, Paul makes this help-ful comment that reaches far beyond that subject alone: "So then we pursue the things which make for peace and the building up of one another" (Rom. 14:19). Those two things go together—peace and building each other up. Words that are designed to encourage others and build them up make for peaceful relationships.

The converse is also true. Seeking the advantage for ourselves causes discord. "For where jealousy and selfish ambition exist, there is disorder and every evil thing" (James 3:16). As long as I am most concerned about my own happiness, my security, my importance, my wellbeing and my self esteem, I will be fighting for the advantage and getting irritable with anybody who tries to put me at a disadvantage. My heart won't change and my words won't get any more pleasant until I establish as my goal building up the other people in my life and strengthening our relationships.

My wife and I tried to play tennis together a few years ago. We thought it would be good exercise, so we went out early several mornings a week to a nearby court. Quite frankly, she was not very good at it. The only way we could keep a volley going was if I lobbed the ball gently to her in the center of the court. But every once in awhile I would exert my male ego and competitive spirit, rush the net, and drive the ball back into one corner or the other to gain the advantage. If I were in some kind of competition, that would have been a good thing. But if I merely wanted to keep a volley going with my wife for the purpose of exercise, it was not very smart. She would try to hit it back, but would usually swing wildly and either miss the ball completely or hit it over the fence. There were times that she got a little irritated with me. We finally decided tennis wasn't such a good idea for us after all.

> **Pursue the things which make for peace.**

Unfortunately, there have been times in our marriage when I have used similar tactics in our relationship. I have tried to gain the advantage by driving her back into a corner with anger, unkindness, accusations, criticism, putdowns, blame, exaggerations, silence, manipulation, incriminating questions, nagging, and a host of other unfair communication techniques. And she has done the same to me, because when we get in a corner ourselves, we usually try to drive the other person back into a corner as well. One of us may have felt like we had won a point now and then, but what value would that have been if, as a result, we had decided to quit playing the game, if we had called an end to our marriage?

That is where some couples are right now. They have given up, or are on the verge of giving up. How unnecessary! If we are both believers in Christ, if we understand our position as children of God and apply the Word of God to our own lives, we can keep ourselves out of the corner of anger, anxiety, guilt, and fear. Then by being committed to building the relationship rather than winning the game, we can keep our partners out of the corners too, in the center of the court, in a position of emotional and spiritual strength where they feel good about themselves and glad they are who they are. Then they can respond to us positively. The result will be that we keep the volley going, that we both learn to play the game better and find a great deal more happiness. That could change our whole outlook on life and keep the sweet water of pleasant words flowing from the fountain. Don't you think it's worth a try?

# 12

# WISE AS
# SERPENTS

ONE DAY THE LORD JESUS called His twelve disciples to Him, gave them supernatural power over demons and disease, and then sent them throughout the land of Israel to minister to needs and to preach the gospel of the kingdom. He said to them, "Behold, I send you forth as sheep in the midst of wolves: be ye therefore wise as serpents and harmless as doves" (Matt. 10:16, KJV). Their serpent-like wisdom would govern the words they spoke as well as the activities they carried out. Jesus wanted them to communicate His message wisely, but without hurting the people who heard it. They were to be as harmless as doves.

Solomon linked wisdom with words hundreds of years earlier. In Proverbs 16:23 he said, "The heart of the wise instructs his mouth." True wisdom affects the way we speak. Again, "The tongue of the wise makes knowledge acceptable" (Prov. 15:2).

A person may have a head full of knowledge, but wisdom helps his tongue to express it in an appropriate and acceptable way. "... but the tongue of the wise brings healing" (Prov. 12:18). God's wisdom, expressed through the tongue, results in healing rather than harm, just as the Lord Jesus said.

Some folks consider themselves to be wise, but their words hurt rather than heal. That leads us to believe there is another kind of wisdom besides God's, and the apostle James confirmed that. James, like Solomon, linked wisdom to the way we use our tongues. Immediately after twelve verses on the tongue, he wrote, "Who among you is wise and understanding? Let him show by his good behavior his deeds in the gentleness of wisdom" (James 3:13). He is talking about our entire manner of life, not just words. But we cannot eliminate words from what he said. He goes on to mention bitter jealousy and selfish ambition (v.14), things which are normally expressed by destructive communication. "For where jealousy and selfish ambition exist, there is disorder and every evil thing" (James 3:16). Unwise words harm rather than heal.

**Unwise words harm rather than heal.**

We may think we have used good sense and sound judgment in what we have said, but if it has produced disorder, dissension, and turmoil rather than healing, it has not been God's wisdom, but rather a counterfeit wisdom. "This wisdom is not that which comes down from above, but is earthly, natural, demonic" (James 3:15). It finds its source in one of three places: in earthbound motives, in our old sinful natures, or in Satan himself.

You really don't want that kind of wisdom, do you? I would assume you want the real thing, wisdom from above, wisdom that helps and heals, that brings peace and harmony, that increases love and good feelings among God's people. How can we know whether our words are prompted by godly wisdom or by counterfeit wisdom? James gives us a sevenfold standard by which to measure them. "But the wisdom from above is first pure, then peaceable, gentle, reasonable, full of mercy and good fruits, unwavering, without hypocrisy" (James 3:17). Let us weave that standard into the fabric of our thinking so that we too can be wise as serpents, yet harmless as doves.

## Wise Words Are Pure

It is no accident that James said, "first, pure." He means exactly that. First and foremost, the wisdom that comes from God must be pure. The word *pure* was originally applied by ancient Greek writers to the supposed purity of the pagan gods, but later it came to describe the purity necessary to approach these gods—not just outward ceremonial purity, but purity of heart. That is the way the New Testament writers used it. Wise words come from a pure heart, pure in every sense of the word, a heart that has been cleansed of error, moral impurity, bitter jealousy, selfish ambition, and ulterior motives. Our words are a reflection of what goes on inside us, so if our

> **Good communication begins with a cleansed heart.**

hearts are impure, our words will ultimately betray us. We may be able to fake it for a while, but eventually the truth will be known. Good communication begins with a cleansed heart.

How can we get our hearts cleaned up? The Bible portrays them as deceitful and desperately wicked (Jer. 17:9). It is obvious that this is no self-help reformation project. It demands radical divine intervention. That is exactly what God did when He sent His Son to earth to die in our place. Basically and fundamentally, it is the blood of Jesus Christ that cleanses our hearts of sin (1 John 1:7). When we acknowledge our sinful condition and place our trust in Christ and His death for us at Calvary, God applies the cleansing power of His blood to our lives. He purifies us and removes our guilt.

The assurance that we are clean, that our sins are forgiven, and that God has accepted us, becomes the basis for wise words.

It frees us from the need to demean others in order to compensate for the guilt we feel over our own shortcomings. Our burden of guilt is gone! It frees us from the need to make ourselves look good, or to have our own way, or attain our own ambitions in order to prove that we really are worthwhile people. We know we are of value in Christ. It frees us from the perverted attempt to appear sophisticated by using impure speech. The more we understand of the debt Christ paid and the greater appreciation we develop for the magnitude of God's grace, the wiser and purer our communication will become.

## Wise Words Are Peaceable

Now that our relationship with God is settled, we are ready to deal with our relationship with others. "Then peaceable," James says. It must be in that order. "Then" is a word that clearly indicates succession of order. Once we trust Christ, we have two advantages. First, we have the assurance that God has wiped the slate of our lives clean. We are forgiven and accepted. And second, we have the supernatural power of His indwelling Holy Spirit to help us communicate wisely. He enters our lives and enables us to express the wisdom of God in our words and actions. When we allow Him to do that, our words will be peaceable.

> The person who is filled with God's wisdom is not easily provoked into arguing.

The person who is filled with God's wisdom is not easily provoked into arguing. He isn't quarrelsome or contentious, but consistently seeks a peaceful solution to the problem. He believes that strong, loving relationships are more important than winning arguments. He takes the exhortation of Paul seriously: "If possible, so far as it depends on you, be at peace with all men" (Rom. 12:18). He weighs his words carefully, and endeavors to phrase them in such a way as to avoid arousing antagonism in others. If others attack him with angry, exaggerated accusations, he refrains from responding in kind, but calmly seeks to understand their needs and what He can do to help them. He is a peacemaker, whom Jesus called a true son of God (Matt. 5:9). He knows how to avoid arguments and solve conflicts.

Jack is a man who is growing in God's wisdom. He still has his faults, however, as we all do, and one of them is his failure to help his wife at those times when she is overwhelmed with her responsibilities—the burden of housework, caring for their three small children, and acting as the superintendent of the Primary Department of the Sunday school. When she chides him about his indifference, he gets angry and cool toward her. But one night he was thinking about how much he loves her and appreciates her, and how much he wants her to know it. So while she was at her departmental meeting at church, he not only put the kids to bed, but cleaned up the kitchen and vacuumed the house.

When she came home she was temporarily stunned and blurted out rather foolishly, "I hope you don't think that makes up for all the times you left it for me to do." There was a time when words like that would have precipitated an angry argument with counter accusations being hurled at each other long into the night. But Jack is learning about the peaceable wisdom from above, so he said, "No, this doesn't even begin to make up for all those times. I just want you to know that I love you and that I'm going to try to be more sensitive to your needs. I hope this is just a small beginning." Not only did the rest of the evening go beautifully, but their relationship was strengthened. Wise words are peaceable.

## Wise Words Are Gentle

*Gentle* is a difficult word to render into English. There is not one English word that sums it up adequately. If refers to a mild, gentle, and kind forbearance that refrains from insisting on the letter of the law, a gracious, yielding spirit that refrains from tenaciously standing up for one's own rights. A gentle person recognizes that there are more important things than rules and regulations, namely people and relationships. And while he may have the right and the power to enforce the law, he tempers strict justice with mercy.

A gentle person bends in consideration of other people's feelings. He makes allowances for their weaknesses. He lets them be human. He knows the importance of "going by the book," but he also knows that the people and the circumstances involved may warrant an exception to the book once in a while. Since he doesn't insist on the letter of the law, he is usually the first to ask forgiveness of someone with whom he has quarreled, even if the other person was more wrong than he was. And he has a way of forgetting the wrongs committed against him rather than storing them up to use in a future confrontation.

Let me tell you about Sue, a woman who is growing in the gentleness of God's wisdom. She had been terribly hurt when several of her friends at church turned against her and began excluding her from their morning coffee session. Rumors of unkind things they were saying about her kept filtering back. She was tempted to tell her pastor what they were doing but realized that her motives were basically to put them in a bad light, so she decided against that. Instead, she went to them one by one in meekness and asked how she had offended them. Their complaints were petty, but she sincerely apologized for each one, and in her heart she fully forgave them for their unkindnesses to her.

> **The wisdom from above is always open to consider the other person's point of view.**

In the days that followed, she treated each one of them with genuine respect and love. Her gentleness was rewarded when one of them came to her for advice on handling a problem with her children, and all of them began to reach out to her once more. Human wisdom would say, "Let everybody know what those gossiping ladies are like." Sue had the right and the power to do that, but she didn't. She let gentleness prevail, and it contributed to better relations between God's people.

## Wise Words Are Reasonable

The King James Version says "easy to be entreated," and that explains this word rather well. But it is only one word in the Greek text, so either *reasonable, conciliatory, yielding* or *submissive* might be acceptable English equivalents. The reasonable person is not stubborn or inflexible, but pliable, ready to listen to reason, willing to yield to reasonable requests or opinions. There are professing Christians who, once they make up their minds, simply do not want to be confused with any more facts. They refuse to moderate or alter their stand no matter how much new light is presented, or how many people disagree. That is not God's wisdom. It is human wisdom at best, devilish wisdom at worst. The wisdom from above is always open to consider the other person's point of view.

Few things are more detrimental to good relationships than the attitude of a person who thinks he is always right. If you see it one way, he will probably see it another. And the possibilities of his ever changing his mind are slim indeed. You either give in to him or live with the constant friction of open disagreement. Compromises are out of the question for him. You play by his rules or you don't play at all. People like that rarely understand why others back away from them, and they may keep on insisting that they are right until their last friend is gone.

Is it possible that you could be operating on human wisdom in this area? Ask your wife, your husband, your children, or some acquaintances whether they view you as reasonable. Then ask God to fill you with His wisdom—wisdom that listens to reason.

## Wise Words Are Full of Mercy and Good Fruits

There are two ideas here, but they go together. True wisdom is filled with mercy—feelings of sympathy and compassion toward people who are suffering. But mercy does not stop with the feelings. It causes us to speak words of kindness and encouragement, then do something to help relieve the suffering. James wanted to be sure we understood that. That is probably why he added, "and good fruits." God's wisdom working through us extends practical help to others in need, even to people who have wronged us. That is an element of mercy we find difficult to express.

Real mercy restrains the urge to get even, then goes one step further and reaches out in kindness to help. Sue, the woman we met who was gentle, would also have been full of mercy and good fruits had she cooked a meal for one of those women who had hurt her when the woman and her family were down with the flu. Wisdom like that will go a long way toward overcoming conflicts with others. People who overlook little slights and keep reaching out to help one another with acts of kindness will have very little problem maintaining harmonious relationships.

> **Real mercy restrains the urge to get even, then goes one step further and reaches out in kindness to help.**

## Wise Words Are Unwavering

This aspect of God's wisdom helps us stand firm on biblical principles and undivided in our allegiance to Him. But it also keeps us from vacillating according to the expediency of the moment in our relationships with each other. The person with human wisdom is shifty. He may speak well of a person one day but cut him down the next, whichever is to his advantage. He may insist that one course of action is best today but insist on the very opposite tomorrow, whichever is to his advantage. He may assure you that what he is doing is legal, but if his competitor does it, he will tell you that it is dishonest. He may let his children engage in certain behavior one day but not the next, because it happens to get on his nerves more then. He can usually justify his contradictions with irrefutable logic, but it is wavering human wisdom, prompted by pride and selfishness. And it harms his relationships rather than healing and strengthening them. God's wisdom is consistently fair, reasonable, and considerate of others.

## Wise Words Are Without Hypocrisy

The word *hypocrite* was used originally of Greek actors on the stage, people who could play a role expertly, often wearing masks. But it came to be applied to anyone who covered up his true self and pretended to be something he was not. That is what human wisdom does. It is deceptive, evasive, and clever at concealing its real character, aims, and motives. The person who uses it answers you in ambiguous and confusing terms so you cannot pin him down and know exactly what he is like, what he is thinking or what he is after. He lives with his guard up and his mask on, seldom letting you know what he is really feeling. It is nearly impossible to develop any kind of mutually satisfying interpersonal relationship with him.

The wisdom from above is the very opposite of that. It is open, honest, and straightforward. The person who has it does not try to disguise his feelings to make himself look good or gain his own ends. If he is disturbed about something, he says so, kindly but honestly. He doesn't say, "No, there's nothing wrong between us" just to avoid the unpleasantness of confrontation or to cover up his pickiness. He shares his feelings openly, without criticizing or finding fault with others, and so helps to keep the channels of communication open. He contributes to an atmosphere of peace and harmony, and that is the kind of atmosphere in which righteousness can grow. James concludes this chapter about words by reminding us that the peacemaker who sows in peace reaps the fruit of righteousness (James 3:18).

Will you ask God for His wisdom? He makes it available to you freely and abundantly (see James 1:5). When you have it, your words will be wise, your relationships will be peaceful, and righteousness will abound.

# 13

# ACTIONS SPEAK
# LOUDER THAN WORDS

BEING FULLY HUMAN, and possessing a thoroughly sinful nature that I inherited from Adam, I have found myself deciding on occasion that I would not communicate with my wife. Although they were always foolish decisions, I thought I had good reason. She had misunderstood what I was trying to say (on purpose, I felt), misrepresented my intentions, misjudged my motives or accused me unjustly, and I thought the safest thing for me to do was to clam up. It's a game many of us play. Subconsciously we think the silent treatment will punish those who have treated us unfairly. Maybe it will cause them to react in some extreme way, further justifying our self-righteous insistence that they were wrong all along.

I have since learned, however, that I was actually communicating by my silence. My actions were saying something to my wife, something like, "I don't care about your feelings. My feelings are more important than yours. And furthermore, you can't treat me that way without paying for it." I didn't consciously desire to communicate that message. My conscious thought was to protect myself from further hurt. I really loved her and wanted to be close to her. But that's not what came through to her.

> **Communication does not occur through words alone.**

You see, what we do or fail to do says something. It is practically impossible not to communicate when we are in the presence of another person. Communication does not occur through words alone. Communication is any behavior which someone else interprets as bearing a message. We speak with our posture, our gestures, our face, our eyes, our eyebrows. We speak with a sigh, a touch, a tone, a shoulder shrug. We speak with the distance we put between us and another person, in fact with almost any action we take. Experts tell us that 65 percent or more of all our communication is nonverbal. They also tell us that nonverbal messages are more powerful than verbal messages.

If we send two messages which contradict each other, people will have a tendency to believe the nonverbal over the verbal. For instance, if I tell you that I believe what you are telling me but my jaw is tight, my head is tilted, and there is a deep frown on my brow, you will probably conclude that I don't believe you at all. Actions really do speak louder than words! And that is why it is so very important for us as Christians to be aware of our actions and to make sure that what we do is consistent with what we say.

The Bible makes this emphasis. For example, John wrote, "But whoever has the world's goods, and sees his brother in need and closes his heart against him, how does the love of God abide in him? Little children, let us not love with word or with tongue, but in deed and truth" (1 John 3:17–18). If we say we love another believer but let him go on suffering when we have the ability to relieve his suffering, we don't love him at all. Our actions contradict our words, and actions speak louder than words.

James made a similar observation. "If a brother or sister is without clothing and in need of daily food, and one of you says to them, 'Go in peace, be warmed and be filled,' and yet you do not give them what is necessary for their body, what use is that? Even so faith, if it has no works is dead, being alone" (James 2:15–17). We can say we know the Lord, but if we are indifferent to the needs of other Christians, our actions contradict our words, and actions speak louder than words.

As we have seen, James moves from that exhortation on living faith into a major discourse on words which he concludes by asking, "Who among you is wise and understanding? Let him show by his good behavior his deeds in the gentleness of wisdom" (James 3:13). Although we cannot divorce words from that exhortation, it does refer primarily to nonverbal communication. Wise Christians let their manner of life back up what they say with their mouths. And they do it with the meekness or gentleness of wisdom, that is, without contentiousness, without arrogance, without self-centeredness, and without retaliation against those who have wronged them. They do it with a gentle friendliness and unselfish consideration of others.

> **If we send two messages which contradict each other, people will have a tendency to believe the nonverbal over the verbal.**

When James described the true wisdom that comes from God, he said it is "without hypocrisy." One way to characterize people whose actions contradict their words is "hypocritical." They are inconsistent, professing something by their words which they do not possess in their hearts. It is important for the wise Christian to act in a manner consistent with his words, and it is important for at least three reasons.

## For Harmonious Relationships

Harmony is uppermost in James' mind. He talks about peacemakers who sow in peace (James 3:18), and then moves directly into a discussion of quarrels and conflicts (4:1). There seems to be in his mind a correlation between harmonious relationships and consistency between words and deeds. Some counselors feel that failure to heed this principle is one of the major causes for interpersonal strife and marital casualties. They are confident that many of the problems which develop in a relationship could be worked out simply by dealing with the inconsistencies between verbal and nonverbal messages.

> **It is important for the wise Christian to act in a manner consistent with his words.**

For example, a husband may assure his wife that he loves her, yet he is often late coming home from work and seldom calls to inform her. When she questions him, he insists that he had to work late, or run an errand, or see a friend, or something. She explains to him that it is important for her to know when he will be late so she can plan dinner accordingly. But he fails to call again and again, and meal after meal is spoiled. While his words say, "I love you," his actions say, "I couldn't care less about your wishes or your feelings. "And she believes the actions above the words. Her human tendency is to become indignant, then resentful, and eventually indifferent to his wishes and feelings. Any hope of intimacy they might have cherished is dashed on the rocks of bickering and arguing.

Or turn it around. A wife tells her husband that she wants to do everything she can to ensure his happiness, but she never cooks him his favorite meal. He asks her to prepare it for him and she assures him she will do it someday when she has the proper ingredients and the time, but she never does. Whenever he mentions it, she says, "Please don't bug me about it. I'll fix it when I can get around to it." But months pass by and she still hasn't done it. Her actions say, "Your happiness is the least of my concerns," and soon he begins to believe the actions above the words. Again, resentment begins to poison the relationship and pour fuel on their fiery arguments.

It isn't normally the big things that bring a marriage to the brink of collapse. It is the accumulation of little acts that have convinced each of them that the other really does not care. No protests of love will be able to convince them otherwise, because actions speak louder than words.

> **Actions speak louder than words.**

The principle does not only affect marital relationships. It affects every relationship of life. For example, believers are encouraged to "rejoice with those who rejoice and weep with those who weep" (Rom. 12:15). That is a natural byproduct of our love for one another and our care for one another in the body of Christ.

So a woman comes into a ladies group and she is bubbling over with joy. "I'm so excited. My husband trusted Christ as his Savior last night!" And the ladies in the circle say, "Oh, that's nice," as they sit motionless with arms folded, legs crossed and somber faces. I can guarantee you that the woman with the newly born-again husband is not going to feel a closeness or intimacy with those ladies, nor any desire to share her heart with them. Their actions contradict their words.

The same thing applies to the man who loses his job. When he tells a friend at church his distressing news, his friend replies, "That's too bad, Tom. I'm sorry to hear it." Then he immediately turns away to ask another friend what time they are supposed to leave on their fishing trip tomorrow morning. He never enquires of Tom about his search for a new job, nor does he ever ask him what he can do to help. As you might suspect, Tom starts attending another church where the actions of the people are consistent with their words. It is difficult to enjoy a satisfying and harmonious relationship with people who do not confirm their words with their actions.

## For Successful Instruction

There is a second reason that our actions must match our words, and that is to be an example to those we endeavor to teach, and so to enhance their potential for learning. The "Do As I Say But Not As I Do" philosophy is a total educational disaster. The most successful learning takes place when the student sees a positive example of what is being taught. That was the method the Lord Jesus used with His disciples. They probably learned more by watching Him than by listening to Him. For example, the night He taught them to serve one another in humility and love, He assumed the role of a servant and washed their dirty feet. They learned more from that dramatic object lesson than they could possibly have learned from a sermon alone.

> **The most successful learning takes place when the student sees a positive example of what is being taught.**

On several occasions the apostle Paul exhorted his converts to follow his example (see 1 Corinthians 4:16; 11:1; Philippians 3:17; 4:9). He modeled through his actions the truth he taught with his lips. He likewise challenged Timothy to be an example to the believers to whom he ministered (1 Tim. 4:12), and encouraged Titus to do the same (Titus 2:7). It is foolish to try to teach someone else to do something when we do the very opposite ourselves.

We parents are probably most guilty of that brand of hypocrisy. We want our children to learn to talk to us in kind and quiet tones rather than scream at us. We explain that to them clearly and simply. But five minutes later they hear Mom screaming at Dad, "How many times have I told you not to throw that dirty sweatshirt on the dining room table?" Or worse yet, one of them is screaming at the kids, "I've told you kids a thousand times not to scream at me while I'm talking on the telephone." The words are meaningless. We teach far more by our actions than by our words.

> **We teach far more by our actions than by our words.**

Take another example. Both Mom and Dad have tried to teach the kids to carry out their responsibilities willingly and cheerfully rather than with a complaining spirit. But one evening mom says to dad, "Dear, I'd like you to fix the leaky faucet in the kitchen tonight. We're wasting a lot of water." Dad has had an exceptionally trying day at work, and fixing a leaky faucet is the last thing in the world he wants to do. He should have said kindly and forthrightly, "Not tonight, honey. Tomorrow's Saturday and I'll get it first thing in the morning." But he suspects that he will get a hassle if he does that, so instead he answers rather grumpily, "All right. All right—in a minute." An hour later he gets up and goes out to the garage, slamming the door so hard it shakes the whole house. He is heard grumbling about the mess the kids left on the workbench. Then he grumbles about the design of the faucet which makes the job twice as difficult to do. And he "accidentally" breaks one of Mom's favorite glasses that was left in the sink. The kids haven't learned much about willingness and cheerfulness.

How we do what we do may be more important than the very doing of it. That's an important lesson to teach children. But they will learn it best by observing it in us. We can stow our words if we are not going to model them

> **How we do what we do may be more important than the very doing of it.**

before our children, because they will copy what they see far more readily than they will follow the instruction they hear. Actions speak louder than words.

There is another form of nonverbal communication we should mention, particularly when talking about teaching children, and that is touching. We want our children to know we love them, but words alone will not convince them. They need to be tenderly touched. Infants who have been deprived of physical contact have actually died as a result. Children who have had no tender caressing have become deeply disturbed. Every human being needs to be touched, apart from any sexual connotations, by those close to him. Husbands and wives need it. And children cannot progress normally without it. A tender touch says, "I love you. You are precious to me." And we learn best from those whom we know care for us.

## For an Effective Testimony

There is at least one more reason why wise Christians must back what they say with what they do, and that is for the sake of the lost who are watching. If they know we are Christians, they are probably observing everything we do. And everything we do communicates something. What are they reading in us? Paul called the Corinthians a letter known and read by all men (2 Cor. 3:2). We are all living letters which the world reads daily. What is your mail saying?

> If we tell an unbeliever that God loves him, we need to show him God's love by the way we treat him.

To the Colossians, Paul says, "Conduct yourselves with wisdom toward outsiders, making the most of the opportunity" (Col. 4:5). That refers to our manner of life, our behavior, our actions. But in the very next verse he talks about words: "Let your speech always be with grace, as though seasoned with salt, so that you may know how you should respond to each person" (4:6). We cannot separate our words from our actions. They must be consistent with each other. If we tell an unbeliever that God loves him, we need to show him God's love by the way we treat him.

One family decided that they would adopt as their project the showing of Christ's love to an unsaved neighbor family. They prayed together for the family. The kids shared their toys with their kids. Dad volunteered to help their dad put in a sprinkler system. Mom took food over when they lost a relative. Their consistent expression of love opened the door to a verbal witness, and the family came to know Christ. That was conducting themselves with wisdom toward outsiders. And it was their actions more than their words that brought the family to Christ.

> **Do we talk to the store clerk with any more kindness than the unbeliever does?**

We can tell our non-Christian acquaintances that Christ makes a difference in our lives, but they will pay more attention to our actions. Do we talk to the store clerk with any more kindness than the unbeliever does? Are we any more inclined to help a stranger in distress? Do we handle inconveniences with more calmness? Do we receive bad news with more peace and control? Do we treat our families with more unselfish consideration?

The world is watching. Wise Christians will show by their good behavior their deeds in the gentleness of wisdom (James 3:17). The only way we can do that is by immersing ourselves in the person of Jesus Christ, occupying our thoughts with Him and His Word, letting Him capture our affection, control us completely, and live through us. Then the hypocrisy will be gone and others will know that we are real—our families, friends, fellow-workers, as well as the unbelievers around us. And they will begin to believe our words.

> **The world is watching.**

# 14

# WHO'S LISTENING?

IT IS FASCINATING TO WATCH a young couple in love. They have no problem communicating with each other, talking excitedly and enthusiastically by the hour. There are times when they both seem to be talking at once and we wonder who is listening. The fact of the matter is, they are both listening. They each seem to be such skilled communicators that they have an uncanny ability to talk and listen at the same time.

Then they get married and something changes. They begin to feel as though they have heard most of the interesting things the other has to say, or that they know most everything about the other there is to know. And quite frankly, they are not quite sure they like what they hear the other saying. So listening isn't nearly as easy, exciting, or important as it used to be. It doesn't come automatically as it once did. Now it is work. It takes time and energy that they may not be willing to give. It is an art that must be continually cultivated and developed. They begin to lose the motivation and the inclination to listen to each other. And again we wonder who is listening.

As the old story goes, there was a time when he talked and she listened. On their honeymoon she talked and he listened. And now that they are settled down in their own home, they both talk and the neighbors listen. And if they don't yell loud enough for the neighbors to hear, maybe nobody's listening.

The problem exists not only in marriage. Our failure to listen to one another in all walks of life is one of our most serious hindrances to good interpersonal relationships. We can be looking someone straight in the eye, nodding agreement and grunting "Uh huh" while our minds are miles away—perfecting a golf swing, fretting over a lost contract, worrying about yesterday's report from the doctor, hunting tigers on an African safari, planning tomorrow's dinner, or any one of thousands of options. We give only superficial attention to what is being said, or we miss it altogether.

> **Our failure to listen to one another is one of our most serious hindrances to good interpersonal relationships.**

Let's face it, most of us would rather talk than listen. We consider listening to be a temporary and unpleasant interlude between opportunities to say what we want to say. Instead of giving attention to what others are saying, we often are thinking about what we are going to say next, either to amaze and amuse our friends or to confound and convince our opponents. The result may be conversation, but it is not communication. We may be in a group, but we are not functioning as individuals. There is no true fellowship taking place. We are not learning to know each other better so we can minister more effectively to each other's needs. We are just a group of isolated islands, each one crying out for someone to listen and to care. We can only build bridges to other people when we listen. We have said a great deal in this book about talking. Let's give some attention to the art of listening.

> **Let's give some attention to the art of listening.**

## The Obstacles to Listening

Admittedly, listening is hard work. Some people speak so slowly we want to drag their words out of them. We think five times faster than the average person can speak, and that intensifies the problem of listening. Others speak so rapidly that they run their words together and we cannot understand them. Some speak so softly we can't hear them. Others speak so loudly we're embarrassed to be near them. Some talk about things that are irrelevant or illogical. Others drone on about trivial and insignificant matters that bore us. Some can't seem to say what they mean. Others don't know when to wrap it up. All in all, listening can be a drag.

Most of us could be more considerate of others when we speak and not abuse the favor they extend to us when they give us a listening ear. But those very people who are most difficult to listen to may be the ones who most need a listener, and God may be asking us to be those listeners. There are some things we cannot do, but if we have at least one functioning ear, we ought to be able to listen.

One of the greatest obstacles we will have to overcome in our quest to become good listeners is our early training and subsequent habits. As children, we may have been told to be quiet, to stop interrupting, to go away because Mommy and Daddy had no time to listen. And we got the idea that grownups don't have to listen. Studies of school children have revealed that listening declines with each successive grade. It seems as though the older we get, the more we have on our minds to hinder our listening.

It also seems as though the older we get, the more we allow ourselves to be distracted by external factors—people walking by, noises, time pressures, the speaker's personal appearance or annoying mannerisms. I can remember talking frequently to someone who would ask after every few sentences, "Do you know what I mean?" I found myself thinking more about that idiosyncrasy than about what he was saying.

> **The older we get, the more we have on our minds to hinder our listening.**

Sometimes listening can be threatening to us. We fear that we may hear some criticism of ourselves that we would rather not have to confront, some change that we would rather not make, or some demand that we would rather not meet. We may hear an idea that challenges some precious opinion of ours that we would rather not give up. Our best defense is to stop paying attention. We may simply feel that it will take too much effort to understand what is being said to us, so we take the easy way out and turn off our mental hearing aids. It is too much trouble to listen, so why bother?

Why bother? That is a good question. Let's try to answer it.

## The Motive for Listening

If I were to suggest one good reason for cultivating the art of listening, it would be found in 1 John 4:7: "Beloved, let us love one another, for love is from God; and every one who loves is born of God and knows God." Listening is an important and necessary expression of love. Love is giving of ourselves unselfishly, sacrificially, and unconditionally to meet the needs of those to whom it is expressed. And one universal human need is the need to be understood. We want to be assured that somebody knows us, is sensitive to what is happening inside us, feels what we are feeling in the deepest part of our being, and still accepts us and cares for us. It is impossible for anyone to do that except one who truly listens to us. Listening says, "I care about you. You are important enough to invest all the time and effort that is necessary for me to understand you."

So love listens. We can say with our mouths over and over again, "I love you," but it is meaningless unless we are willing to put aside other things and give of ourselves unselfishly to discern the deepest needs of the ones we profess to love. True love is focused on the benefit of others rather than our own benefit, and that means trying to understand them. We all want so desperately to be understood, but God is asking us to take the time to do the understanding.

> **Listening is an important and necessary expression of love.**

Some husbands and wives feel totally misunderstood. They have tried to communicate to their mates their thoughts, feelings, needs, longings, and desires, but they have received little response. Their mates have been too preoccupied with other things such as the newspaper, television, housework, other friends, hobbies, or work. Then one day they meet someone who is genuinely interested in what they have to say, and they allow themselves to be drawn into an intimate relationship. The third party may be less attractive than their mates, but that makes no difference. They think they have met someone who cares, and that fact is of supreme importance to them. It is, however, sin! No rationalization on earth can make it right. It brings with it a new set of problems and heartaches, usually worse than they had before. But that doesn't matter to them. They now feel loved and accepted and understood, and that is what matters most to them. That is the awesome power of the listening ear.

> **The awesome power of the listening ear.**

People will often go to a professional counselor because they know he will listen. It is not that they need advice so much as they need someone who will listen to them with keen interest and undivided attention, someone who will draw them out and help them understand themselves. It doesn't bother them that the counselor costs money. They need that listening ear and they have not been able to find it in their mates or other Christian friends.

I read about a coffee house in San Francisco that has sound-proof booths, where for a stipulated hourly fee a patron will be provided with someone who will listen. Business has been good. People want to talk, express their opinions, give advice, offer quick, easy solutions. But few are willing to take the time to listen and to understand. Understanding a person does not necessarily mean total agreement with him. It means feeling what he is feeling, seeing the situation through his eyes, and sympathizing with him.

> **Understanding a person does not necessarily mean total agreement with him.**

This is one way by which the members of the body of Christ can minister to one another. It is impossible for vocational pastors to meet this need in the life of every believer in a congregation. But we can all minister to one another in this way. We don't need a great deal of training to be good listeners, to ask leading questions, and to encourage people to talk. We just need to do it. By listening, we can bear one another's burdens and so fulfill the law of Christ (Gal. 6:2). By listening, we can demonstrate Christ-like love. Are you willing to try it? If so, you will need to know what it involves.

## The Nature of Listening

The apostle James gave us one of the classic biblical statements on listening. "But let every one be quick to hear, slow to speak and slow to anger" (James 1:19). He had just introduced the subject of God's Word, pointing out that we have been born again by the Word of truth (v. 18), and he is about to encourage us to be doers of the Word and not hearers only (v. 22). So in its context, the verse deals basically with listening to God's Word. Keeping our mouths closed and listening to God's Word will guard us from angrily defending ourselves or denouncing those who disagree with us.

But in this exhortation about God's Word, James has touched on a vital principle of good interpersonal communication. More listening to each other and more thought before we answer will result in less anger and less conflict. So be quick to hear and slow to speak! In other words, make listening a high priority in your life. Do it without delay, without having to be begged; do it with zeal and enthusiasm.

Examining the parallels between listening to God's Word and listening to one another can be quite helpful. To begin with, good Bible study seeks to discover what God means by the words He has revealed, not the meaning we want to attach to them. Good listening does the same. Our aim is to understand what other people mean by the words they use, not what we think they mean or want them to mean. We have a natural tendency to fill their words with meaning colored by our own background, experience, mindset, or preconceived viewpoint, and we need to understand that tendency.

For example, Solomon told his bride her hair was like a flock of goats descending from Mount Gilead (Song of Solomon 4:1). She would have taken that as a compliment. Visualize if you can a large flock of goats descending the distant hillside in a lovely flowing motion. She would understand that. If you tell your wife today that her hair is like a flock of goats, she probably won't speak to you for weeks! She will hear it from her modern-day frame of reference and read all kinds of horrible things into it; unless she understands the biblical picture and is willing to hear your words in that light.

> **Real listening hears people and what they mean, and so builds understanding between them.**

Real listening does not just hear words; it endeavors to understand the meaning of the message intended by the speaker of those words. We may be able to repeat the person's exact words back to him and still not understand their meaning. A parrot can repeat words, but parrots are not very good listeners. Real listening hears people and what they mean, and so builds understanding between them. Isn't that what you would like to do? How then can we be quick to hear?

*Give your undivided attention.* James suggested how we ought to listen to God's Word. "But one who looks intently at the perfect law, the law of liberty, and abides by it, not having become a forgetful hearer but an effectual doer, this man shall be blessed in what he does" (James 1:25). The word *look* means literally "to stoop down beside." There is to be an intensity about the way we search God's Word. We need to listen intently to each other as well. That probably means we will not be able to listen acceptably while we're watching the ball game, reading the newspaper, running the vacuum cleaner, or straightening up the living room. Undivided attention will require eye contact. If we keep looking at other things, glancing at the clock on the wall or tapping our fingers, we are communicating a lack of interest in what is being said. As we have seen, our body language speaks louder than our words. What someone wants to say to us is important enough for us to put aside whatever else we are doing. What a wife wants to say to her husband may even be important enough to warrant his turning off the ball game, as outlandish as that may sound to the average husband. If it is impossible for us to give undivided attention at the moment, then we should set a time when we can, and subsequently follow through with it.

> **Undivided attention will also require us to keep our minds from wandering.**

Undivided attention will also require us to keep our minds from wandering. Just as we are to abide in God's Word, persevere or continue in it (James 1:25), so we should rivet our minds securely to the person who is speaking to us and abide in what he is saying. That may not be easy. We are prone to take mental excursions to places more interesting. But we can discipline ourselves to pay attention if we choose to. Visualizing what the person is saying, putting ourselves in the scene he is describing, or trying to feel what he is feeling will help us sense the importance he attaches to it; visualizing makes it easier for us to concentrate on it.

*Don't interrupt.* "Slow to speak" is also a necessary part of good listening. Oftentimes we think we know what the other person is going to say, so we jump in and finish his sentence for him. Unfortunately, we may miss his point entirely and our interruption only serves to confuse the issue. We may also be quick to express our disagreement or to offer advice before we have fully understood the problem. We have previously referred to Solomon's assessment of that bad habit. "He who gives an answer before he hears, it is folly and shame to him" (Prov. 18:13). Have you seen the poster that says, "If there's one thing I can't stand, it's somebody talking while I'm interrupting"? It may get a chuckle, but probably it reflects a sad slice of reality in our own thinking.

> **If there's one thing I can't stand, it's somebody talking while I'm interrupting.**

We interrupt in more subtle ways as well. Even something as insignificant as a look on our faces can say, "Oh brother, here we go again. How many times do I have to listen to this?" That stifles communication and builds resentment which may someday erupt in conflict. Sometimes we interrupt a conversation in order to do something we think is important, but which *could* wait until later. The telephone has probably cut off more profitable communication in our house than any other single thing. There may be times we should let it ring, or answer it and ask if we can call the party back, or just let the voicemail take it. If God wants us to listen to each other, we will need to put a high priority on doing so.

*Listen non-defensively.* Some of us would rather not listen because we've already made up our minds on the subject. We anticipate some criticism or some demand for change. So we cut the speaker off, change the subject to something more to our liking, or raise our defenses before he ever finishes. That hardly expresses the love of Christ. Just as we should be doers of God's Word and not hearers only, so we should be open to accept new information from other people that differs from our own long-cherished views. We should be willing to consider making changes that God may want us to make. In other words, we should consider doing it as well as hearing it.

We all have traditional ways of thinking and traditional habits that we dearly cherish. We have long been convinced that there is no way but our way, until we are challenged by someone who is convinced that his way is better. In a marital relationship, money is just such a common area of contention. One mate believes the husband should pay the bills, while the other feels that it is perfectly all right for the wife to assume that responsibility. One mate is convinced that every spare penny should be saved. The other feels that after paying the bills and giving to God's work it is acceptable to spend some on family entertainment. They may argue over those issues for years, when an open mind and a non-defensive posture could bring compromise.

**Love does not seek its own.**

Vacations are another notorious area of differences. One loves the mountains while the other loves the beach. One likes to camp while the other prefers to stay in a hotel room where the beds are softer and the water is warmer. One wants to keep on the go and see everything there is to see, while the other wants to stop and relax and do nothing. All attempts to share their feelings or give reasons for their preferences are met with angry resistance and a column of logical arguments. But that is hardly Christ-like love. Love does not seek its own (1 Cor. 13:5). Love not only hears others out without interruption; it is sensitive to their feelings, considerate of their opinions, open to what they say, and willing to consider making changes for their benefit. That says, "I care about you."

If we disagree with what is being said, it might be better to ask for clarification than merely to express our differences immediately, and then try not to give an answer until we are able to communicate the meaning of the other person's statement to his satisfaction. When we finally are able to restate his position in a way that is acceptable to him, we may find that our disagreement has been dissolved. Good listening that asks questions and requests clarification also may help us keep our anger level down, just as James suggested. Being quick to hear and slow to speak will help us also to be slow to anger.

> **Being quick to hear and slow to speak will help us also to be slow to anger.**

*Say something.* Some of us husbands are notorious for not responding at all. We meet our wives' attempts to communicate with total silence. While silent wives seem to be a rarer species, there are some around. We all know that silence may be golden, and there may be times when two people just want to enjoy each other's company without saying a word. Solomon said there is a time to speak and a time to be silent (Eccl. 3:7). But silence as a response to being spoken to can be ambiguous. It could communicate anger, disagreement, or defiance on one hand, but understanding, acceptance or consent on the other. It may mean "I don't think you're worth listening to" or it simply may mean "I don't know what to say." But inevitably it will be interpreted to mean, "I don't care what you're saying." And that hurts. To say *something* will at least let people know we are listening and that we care.

Say something like, "I understand what you are saying." Or "I can appreciate that." Or "It sounds to me like you . . . ," and then recapitulate what you think the other person has said. That is his clue that you are interested and want to hear more. And that is the loving thing to do. When we truly love one another, we won't be asking any longer, "Who's listening?" It will be obvious that we all are listening to one another, that we want to understand each other and get along with one another, and so glorify our Lord.

# ENDNOTES

1   Ed Wheat, *Love Life for Every Married Couple* (Grand Rapids: Zondervan Publishing Company, 1980), p. 126.

2   Ibid., p. 141.

3   See also 1 Timothy 5:20; 2 Timothy 4:2; Titus 1:9, 13; Titus 2:15; and Revelation 3:19.

4   R. Laird Harris, Gleason L. Archer, Jr., and Bruce K. Waltke, *Theological Wordbook of the Old Testament* (Chicago: Moody Press, 1980), 2.475.

5   John Powell, *Why Am I Afraid to Tell You Who I Am?* (Niles, Illinois: Argus Communications, 1969).

6   Alan Loy McGinnis, *The Friendship Factor* (Minneapolis: Augsburg Publishing House, 1979), pp. 93–94.

7   Frank B. Minirth and Paul D. Meier, *Happiness Is a Choice* (Grand Rapids, Michigan: Baker Book House, 1978), p. 150.

8   Alan Loy McGinnis, *The Friendship Factor* (Minneapolis: Augsburg Publishing House, 1979), pp. 159–160.

9   S. I. McMillen, *None of These Diseases* (Old Tappan, New Jersey: Fleming H. Revell, 1967), pp. 70–71.

10  Lawrence J. Crabb, Jr., *Effective Biblical Counseling* (Grand Rapids, Michigan: Zondervan Publishing Company, 1977), p. 59 ff.